DECADENCE
AND OTHER PLAYS

EAST / WEST / GREEK

STEVEN BERKOFF

faber and faber

LONDON · BOSTON

This collection
first published in 1989
by Faber and Faber Limited
3 Queen Square London WC1N 3AU

Decadence and *Greek* were first published privately by the author
in 1981 and 1980 respectively and then in the same volume in 1982
by John Calder (Publishers) Ltd, London.
East was first published in 1977 by John Calder (Publishers) Ltd, London
West was first published in *West and other plays* in 1985
by Faber and Faber Limited.

Printed in England by Clays Ltd, St Ives plc
Photoset by Wilmaset, Birkenhead, Wirral
All rights reserved

A CIP record for this book is
available from the British Library

ISBN 0–571–14073–4

2 4 6 8 10 9 7 5 3

This book is to be returned on or before
the last date stamped below.

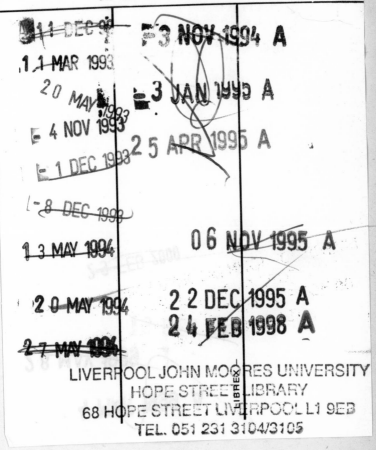

CONTENTS

DECADENCE

For Helen

AUTHOR'S NOTE

Decadence is a study of the ruling classes or upper classes, so called by virtue of strangulated vowel tones rather than any real achievement. The voice is caught in the back of the throat and squashed so as to release as little emotion as possible. Consonants are hard and biting, since emotion is carried on the vowel. The upper class slur the vowel or produce a glottal stop, which by closing down of the glottal creates an impure vowel-like 'hice' for 'house'. They move in awkward rapid gestures or quick jerks and sometimes speak at rapid speeds to avoid appearing to have any feeling for what they say. They achieve pleasure very often in direct relation to the pain they cause in achieving it. Particularly in causing intolerable suffering to achieve exquisite pâtés; boiling lobsters alive with other crustaceans, and hunting down defenceless animals to give them (the hunters) a sense of purpose on Sundays.

These activities can be achieved only by dulling the emotions that spring from awareness, and increasing sadomasochistic activity. Emotion for others, feelings of altruism and generosity, have to be suppressed in order to be able to tolerate the life-style they have adopted. Public schools help to foster the image of superiority without merit and the repression of sensuality. The emphasis being on imposing your will on lesser and junior colleagues, which in turn breeds the future masters and officers class. Upper-class people often regress when in groups to behaviour of simple infantilism, since this is the only time they can escape into their childhood, which was cut off by boarding school at an early age. They are very often seen to be anally fixated, having never made a natural progress into maturity. Equality is an awkward feeling whereas being ruled or ruling produces fluency in speech or actions. Equality suggests that giving should be on an equal par and makes demands that they have not been equipped to deal with. So they make bad lovers but are known to be very decent to servants and extremely loyal to royalty, which to them represents the pinnacle of achievement and the sum total of Englishness.

Decadence was first performed at the New End Theatre, Hampstead, London, on 14 July 1981. The cast was as follows:

HELEN	Linda Marlowe
STEVE	Steven Berkoff
SYBIL	Linda Marlowe
LES	Steven Berkoff
Director	Steven Berkoff

A new production of *Decadence* was presented at Wyndham's Theatre on 25 February 1987.

ACT ONE

SCENE I

*Black floor. A white set. Woman in black. Man in black and white.
A woman sits on a white leather sofa. Music plays, a forties
Ambrose record. A man in tails and wing collar stands near her in a
pose of frozen upper-class glee. He remains frozen until he speaks,
apart from lighting her cigarette. All cigarettes and drinks are mimed
with great emphasis to extract the greatest amount of absurdity from
the physical response. Acting should be sensual, erotic, flamboyant.*

HELEN: How sweet of you to come on time / bastard! sweet
    darling! my you do look so divine. I've been so bored / have
    a drink / what . . . ? / Of course! a Drambuie with soda and
    a splash of Cinzano . . . with masses of ice / I've been so
    bored tearing round to find just what would enchant you to
    eat me for breakfast (*Raising skirt*) charmant n'est-ce pas /
    does it make you go all gooey / does it send spasms up and
    down your spine / enough ice! sweety you do look nice. Do
    you like my legs? / aren't my frillies sweet / does it make you
    get just a little on heat / kiss me / gently / don't smudge
    now / just a touch / a graze won't be a trice / I'll get ready /
    so late I couldn't find a fucking taxi / oh I hate to miss the
    first scene the first embrace / what's that we're seeing / the
    name of the play! / taxis were thin on the ground / outside
    Harrods there were none around / I stretched out an arm / I
    felt like Moses / what did he do / raise his arms to heaven for
    the Hebrews / the longer he kept his arm in the air the better
    would his armies fare, but when it fell wearily down / bloody
    nosed moishers and crunch smash and pound / you've not
    said a word / but you do look dishy / a bird in the ice floes /
    or chilled meringue frappé / you look simply gay / got a fag
    . . . hmm! Smoke gets in your eyes! Shit! Oh sorry / tit!
    Ready heart? Where for dinner after / surprise me then, give
    me a thrill / so long as I gorge on some juicy meat / I'm as
    hungry as a vampire / if I don't eat soon I'll simply expire /
    did you have a nice day / little wife all safe and tucked away /

7

come open your mouth and dazzle my ears / come love
. . . / you look troubled / close to tears / what have I done
. . . shit . . . you look bad / what's the matter hone(y)?

STEVE: So bleeding dextrous / wouldn't you know / too much
bloody ice love / tastes like a crow / you ask me the cause
for my down face / wait till you hear what I have to say /
unzip your ears and let me flood them with verbs and make
your mind a jangle of nerves / the bloody slut got cute /
decided for a hunch to hire a dick with a nose like a Jew / a
private detective in case you're not yet clued / to follow me
here / and now I fear the game's up my dear / the bloody
bitch got wise when too many spunkless nights rolled by /
it made her think that I was not emptying my tea pot in her
old kitchen sink /

HELEN: Oh fuck darling /

STEVE: You've said a mouthful there /

HELEN: Don't worry darling / you've nothing to fear / say your
hard on's taking a small holiday this year / the work and
strain of conning your way in this world sends the cock to
the brain / her jealousies are painted shadows / relieve her
pain / and drop a morsel or two in your old dame / but a
private dick / that's a hell of a game!

STEVE: Too bloody true Helen / my god you're a beaut / a
fabulous sight / I could feast my eyes on you day and
night / let's go out on the town / fuck this dick / let's go
and get tight / but damn this greasy bleeder if he's outside
he'll follow us / there's nowhere to hide / then it's all out /
the evidence clear / he'll tell her all there is needed to hear.

HELEN: Is Chartreuse with pink just too too much / my head is
spinning darling / what did you say / are you sure you're
not fantasizing / did you have a bad day / I don't know
what to wear / help me darling don't just stand there.

STEVE: Let me make it clear / let me shake up the slop that tries
to pretend it's a brain not a mop / my dearest wife Sybil,
this morning she said / if I don't stop whoring I'm just as
well dead / now try and get that in your fucking head! A
divorce and it's ample she has all the clues / photos no

doubt / it will make all the news / cut off / not a penny / as broke as a mouse / no fortune no wages / and she keeps the house / got a light?

HELEN: So what shall we do? Oh Stevie / it's beastly what she does to you / is my seam straight / oh come on darling we mustn't be late /

STEVE: You don't seem to realize this beast is trailing my scent / I can't think / my hard on's getting quite bent / to feel this creature so close on my back / spying, reporting my every track / I can just see him now / can't you / putting two and two together to the bloody cow /

SCENE 2

LES *and* SYBIL (*same actors change attitude and positions*).

LES: So, I followed him to this sumptuous flat / a conspiracy is what I make of that /

SYBIL: Wadya mean a conspiracy? To fucking wot? /

LES: Wak your treasure! Your old man's sticking his nasty in some horrible / birds of a fucking feather ducky stick to fucking gether / these ex-public schools well grounded in making fools of us / the country's pus that welts up from the blood and guts of me and you / you married the runt / when your old dad said at the time / he's just a cad / just after your considerable dough / which dad's sweated his balls off for and now you bunged it to some male whore / set up no doubt in pad / contributed by your not inconsiderable swag / it makes you double choke / this ponce swishes you off your feet / your plates of meat / down Blakes or Tramps or other swishy hole / where half-assed bastards and criminals go / the foul / ignoble mob / odd judge MP and law sniff round the seamy door / liking what's on the other side of the swamp / have a romp / Incognito and hope that what's for dough will taste better than old Flo in curlers / rancid in East Cheam / and when they've had their bit of fun / head home again all nice for

Flo / who's lying in a heap of cream and wax / clutching
Cosmopolitan or other crap / with overfed pussy on her lap.
SYBIL: And I don't want to get like that / thanks love / I feel a
little better now / when I found out / I'll kill the fucking
cow I thought / at first / you know how you do / I cried for
days / right broke up / never dreamed that my dear Steve
would do that to me / the big question is why / ours is not
to reason but to die / that's how I felt / but now I'm calmed
and like the sea all tempest tossed / you're thrown this way
and that / like being screwed if you like by some big black
cat / you can't think for the storm shoved up / but after in
the trough of calm / thoughts that seem wise gather round /
counsel me to nothing rash / be clever Sybil / don't go
mad / the taste is sweet when you're stabbing guts in heat /
but later in cold cell / there's too much time to dwell / but
do it neat / cut off his money and you may as well cut off
his feet / he won't move / he can't / he's helpless like his
kind / no drive within / no chin to take the blows that come
at him /
LES: Attagirl / that's how I like to see you chat / like some
fucking great jungle cat / claws withdrawn ready to pounce
and rip apart this paltry mouse / quiet as death still as a
stone / then pow! Tear his flesh off his bones / that's what
we do / take our time / don't frite the bastard he'll shit his
pipe / let him be forgiven / don't do it again darling / slip
powdered glass in his gin / I seen a guy who swallowed
glass / I seen the blood pour out of his ass and out of his
ears / vomit it up in cups of mashy red / the simple
conclusion / he's better off dead!
SYBIL: You're crazy Les I swear / don't do nothing daft / he
knows about you dear /
LES: What! You've told him about me / shit! Now you've blown
my little fantasy!
SYBIL: He only thinks I hired a private dick / but one familiar
for whom I lick his prick / but I disturbed one day by ill
concealed traces of some sexual play / some love tattoos left
in his flies / he thinks I hired a pair of eyes / not realizing

that I was on to anything more strong than a vibrator when he's on his trips so long / and now I know that those business trips were dirty business to see his trick / greasy joints and my dough to help cream the way / they say money's the best lubricator / no need for K-Y.

LES: You sound just great / I could eat you up / you look like a lioness / I feel like your cub / take your knickers off I wanna fuck /

SYBIL: Tell you the truth / I'd rather have a suck!

SCENE 3

STEVE *and* HELEN (*they melt into the characters as before*).

STEVE: (*Smoking*) Do you know I never saw my old dad / maybe on weekends sometime / or end of term / he'd come over with mum in a Toni perm / prize giving / that was it / I never got nothing / a prize nitwit / then we'd go to lunch / sit in a bloody restaurant / a tight horrid bunch of us / all quite like a church and all the other kids with dads and mums pretending it was such fun to see your mum once in three months / a fiver in your pocket and chin up Steve / write to us Colin / work hard Pete / give us a call when you feel the need / cheers love / the Jaguar bites the gravel and tears away in the dust / hands wave from the back / you bite and gulp / feel tears about to start / they're off to somewhere hot / to Monte Carlo for the season / dad's a whiz at bridge and both of them like to dance but never taught me a game of cards that I might join them in their nights of laughs / that I heard from other rooms / when I in bed all alone would moan / these were the days before public school darling or poofs palace for the sons of fools / when I was still a thing to be shunted around / don't make a sound / don't spoil their play / just laughter from other rooms and wet long days / and then the drive to bloody P. school and farewell home for ever really / you'll love it here he said / rugger, cross-country runs / will make the man of

me / he wants so much to be / see you / spring summer
autumn winter / and each time the absence makes the heart
grow colder / more restrained and still the bloody mid-term
restaurants / you are looking older Steve / and how's the
game / you still wing three quarters? / Here's a fiver / shove
it in your pocket / so when the PT master showed a
friendly eye I warmed to him / and when he put his hand
on my thigh / it didn't feel so bad 'cause I missed dad / or
man / or somehow had / to unite with someone not to feel
sad / so at first it's just a little wank / all friendly / just a
dirty prank / start looking forward to it now and getting
good at it myself / and then one day he asked me to stick it
in / right up his ass / I felt a little queer I must confess but
after it felt fine / just like a cunt / funny that / could be a
juicy tart / if you shut your eyes and put your mind on
snatch well after I opened flies like sardine cans / and
public school / it taught me this / that buggery can be total
bliss / some poor small frightened fag / protect him and
you've got his bum for life / well, so one day headmaster
strolls in when I'm giving head / and says Forsyth / you're
dead / get out this school you filthy scum / I won't have
these things going on / just pack your bags / this is not a
school for fags / he wrote to dad / to say your son likes
nothing better than a schoolboy's bum and would he come
up and collect the scum / you see the school was rife / so
thick in queers you could have cut it with a knife / but dad
was too ashamed to think he sired a bloody poof / and sent
instead the chauffeur down to pick me up / who must have
got wind somehow of my deed / since after driving for
some time / he stopped along a country lane / and said /
you're not to blame / these schools are cesspits of male
vice / but I suppose it is sometimes rather nice / it doesn't
make you bent as a hairpin / to indulge sometimes in a little
sin / I've got two kids your age myself he said / and put his
hand right on my prick / and when it got as hard as rock /
he winked and gave it a bit of a lick / bloody hell he turned
me round and shoved it right up my Khyber pass / fuck

you I thought / I've had enough / so dad said when at
home / you disgust me / you perve / dirty little homo /
reptile and foul bandit for turds / take that / and with his
fist delivered a mighty whack / which missed / since I
boxed somewhat at school and knew a thing or two about
Queensberry rules / I didn't just hold prefects' tools / I had
enough somehow from men / and all my hate welled up for
him / don't do it dad I said / and smashed a right hand on
his nose / which forthwith began to sprout a rose / I then
curled hard my other fist and put it on his jaw / mother
screamed and dad looked very ill / but do you know / it
gave me quite a thrill to beat my dad up / suddenly my
pain just went away / and that was the last time I was gay /
I don't regret it though I'm glad to say / I think the dads of
this world carry a lot of blame . . .

HELEN: So darling / what's new? / You lay back like a cow / all
fat and cuddy and relate the news of your distant past / of
your distress at home with nasty old pa / the tape unwinds /
the story starts afresh / and as you speak you seem to lay
back in a bath / you wallow in a trough of all your suffering
and woe / prattle on / take out a cigarette and . . . go! /
And dad did this to me and that / and he said this to me
and that / and he **never** gave me this or that / when I was
young and needy / little wretch more like and greedy / with
an ego like a hole that never can be filled / until it sucked
the very air from out their mouths / and on and on the
never-ending tape of dad and mum / and why you're like
you are / the scars from wounds that open fresh showing
their tincts of blood / whenever I or other by mishap
should graze that precious weal / that you are not too keen
to heal / that you so covetously keep so you can whine
afresh and weep my dad did this to me / he never took me
to the football match / deprived you pet and mum gave you
a hiding / so you kept your little treasure chest of grief /
that you would open when you want to peck at your old
little pains / and multiply a little grief that lasted seconds
into a bible of woe is me / makes us all read the boring text

and thus excuse yourself of all your crimes / just because life's been so unkind / when you can't think, or grow a little bored with how or what to do / the unused precious energy now feeds on you / frustrated in other words / starts fishing out dead herrings of past hurts / and waves them hot and smelly from their long sojourn. / Throw out these stinking fish / don't use another soul to listen to your ancient threadbare woes / you crave for new fresh birds that can fill chock full / unroll again your scroll of agony for them / and then you want new talents / new assaults to taste because you've nothing more to say / how many ways of cooking that old stew / get on your stomach darling (*She starts massaging his back.*) but live now in the present / perceive what's outside you bring home your tales of raw today / and what I'm feeling now / all the hurts accept / nay welcome since they are fresh fish from the ocean / cut off the past that you drag by a rope like some old ship carrying cargoes of junk and waste then you'll be light, weightless and fast not tied like Ulysses to a mast / afraid to hear unchained the Sirens' blast / afraid of the unknown / kill off the kid and be full grown / with me your sack is empty / so feverishly you scratch at some other unsuspecting pair of ears / till they say ow! Enough! I can't take any more / then on you go / the ancient mariner or wandering Jew who must unload his slops and spew / live in the now / and pain and past will crumble fast in sweet fresh air / like ancient mummies dead for years in darkened vaults just fall apart when light and air expose their fetid lair / don't drag your ma and pa from out their graves to bail you out for all the shit / it's you now boy / if the shoe fits . . .

STEVE: Wear it / it's so true (*He starts to grope her.*)

HELEN: Stop it!

STEVE: Darling . . .

HELEN: Stop it!

STEVE: Darling . . .

HELEN: Stop i i i it!!

STEVE: OK darling.

(They both sit on couch – he looks suitably abashed.)

Truce?

HELEN: *(Silence)*

STEVE: Love you!

HELEN: *(Silence)*

STEVE: Lurve you!

HELEN: *(Silence)*

STEVE: Luurrve yoouu!

HELEN: OK. Love you.

(This continues for a moment more – STEVE *sits back happy and contented.)*

STEVE: Mustn't feel sorry for myself / but I do get bored darling waiting for you / to come home and cheer me up / give me a laugh / you're super jolly good at that / not bloody half / a sense of humour / that's a treat / that's what is vital to our love / I think / can't bear humourless people / the ones who think, the ones who think their shit don't stink / still you're right about me love / you've hit it on the nail I do repeat the same old tale / I think I told that story every time / to every different woman of mine / and like a player on the stage / repeating the same life every day / repetition wears the brain away / what's my stars say? Any fortune or some fame along the way / some foreign travel . . . what! My love life is so perfect so there's nothing there / couldn't be better poppet / love you darling / my super wondrous piece of dolly arse / my dishy lovely slice of peach Melba / pour me a gin and it / no make it a Scotch and dry / I fancy that / and then / no parties anywhere tonight / ring Alex would you or old Keith / he'll have a rubber or gin rummy going / bless him, he's a card / raced his Ferrari last week 'gainst Claude's Lamborghini and both bloody collided / pissed myself laughing / you think Keith gave a fart / no fear / that's fucking fixed that one / let's go and get another / and damn me if the blighter didn't just go and buy a bloody new one / what a card / there's too much bloody ice in here you wicked nymph / it takes so long to

train them nowadays / what's for dinner darling /
something new / surprise me / I'm so bloody bored with
filet / tastes like rubber nowadays / what's in the bloody
feed I wonder, plastic chippings I've no doubt / oh let's
book up at Fred's / that's very you / a sole *bonne femme* or
Strogonoff or even a fondue / another drink my sweet / love
you darling / you OK? / You seem a little pinched / what's
up my lollipop eh? / What's a-matter little lollipop / does
you want papa to take your little drawers down and pin you
to the sofa / oh don't look like that / like I'm something
just brought in by the cat / OK I'm off the beam tonight
but feel a little twitchy down there / thought to pass the
time . . . *n'est-ce pas* / *petit divertissement* / no? / That's just
fine with me / lovely legs you've got / they go right up and
up and get lost up your bum / ooops mustn't get a hard
on / just when we are going out / eh love / fancy a tickle
with the old giggle stick / no, OK / you used to get weak at
the knees just at the suggestion / cream your jeans / you
used to say / I suppose you take me now for granted, eh! /
But I'm so bloody bored tonight / don't know the cause /
maybe I'm reaching male menopause / what do you think? /
I'm only joking dear / don't look like you smell some awful
stink.

SCENE 4

Lights fade. Come up on SYBIL *and* LES.

SYBIL: So how's the plot / what's happening / what's the plan /
   are you still with me my desperate Dan / powdered glass or
   poison in his drink / what's better / what do you think? /
LES: It's hard to tell / fuck only knows / poison leaves traces in
   his gut / and clues that may point back to you my pet /
   don't make things worse by sewing seeds that may sprout
   later as evil deeds that tend to boomerang and whack you
   down / kick out the bastard / get rid of the clown / that's
   my advice / get your mouth round that.

DECADENCE

SCENE 5

Mood is from prior scene. Lights fade – come up on HELEN *and*
STEVE.

STEVE: I don't know why I'm so bored /

HELEN: Oh let me cheer you up.

STEVE: Would you?

HELEN: It's very simple – you're a pup who needs a game to
keep his spirits all /

STEVE: Yeees!

HELEN: I'll tell you a story – once upon a time / you just lie
there and I'll be Scheherazade / let me beguile your ears
with tales to ravish you my dear /

STEVE: Let's have a cigarette first.

HELEN: OK.

(*They light cigarettes and they both have hysterical fun blowing
smoke rings.*)

The morning's sun was high up in the sky / a great big
orange in a sea of blue / and caw caws from the fluffy
floating gulls, and yachts were thick as icing in the
breathless still and crispy morning / the wind as soft as
shantung whispers / the windows from my hotel room lay
open and the curtains softly waved from time to time / the
bed as white as arctic snows and little bells would tinkle
from the yachts to tickle in your ears and wake you up / the
servants softly tread down corridors thick pile with chink
of coffee cups and clutching morning papers thickly
folded / little gentle taps on doors / the knuckle's light
morse code to wake the wealthy from their night-long doze,
while swallowed in silk sheets and thick duvets in darkened
curtained rooms they lay / fat and white giant slugs,
stirring with parched and furry mouth anxious for their
morning cups / the room still drenched in the stale cigar
smoke while their stomach's lining burn in torment still
from last night's bloated fill / mignon stuffed with oysters /
cavier and crêpe Suzette, lobster Thermidor and poisoned
liver of wild ducks / the brains of pigs in aspic laced with

17

the tongue of sheep in the blood of nightingales / garlic
crushed in veal whose occupants were shut in boxes from
their birth and fed with milk to be more tender / their flesh
so soft it hurts / so in their fat cocoons they lay in half
somnolent daze / the bathroom scattered like jewels with
multitudes of coloured pills / the clothes lay in a heap, my
watch from Cartier. Good time it keeps / lay on the side /
with a glass of champagne, half drunk, warm and tacky
now / all that had been so sweet the night before / looked in
the morning like death and gore / the plates not gathered
by room service looked a foul and fetid mess / and then the
servant bless him all crisp and white came like an angel / a
blessed sight / a soft tap on the door / like a whisper / like a
plea / to be allowed to serve the tea / and not disturb /
come in I said and lay your treasures by my bed / your
silver tray and pot all steaming hot / and croissants crisp
and soft and twirls of butter / coloured sugar like broken
glass / honey and the *Paris Match* / he gathered up the last
night's dregs and cleared the room / made it sweet and
clean again / removed the clues of last night's greed when
guts were stuffed with sensual things / and then I
breathed / to pay him for his chore / to give a tip I turned
around to wake the bore / the beast I came with / but he
was dead asleep / I could not find a franc for the young and
pretty man / so there he stood like some Apollo waiting to
be dismissed but still stood near the bed / like he was
waiting for a gentle kiss / the tray he held so tight / his
knuckles went quite white / stood in humble supplication /
ready to spin on his heel and exit at my will / I raised a
hand / just enough to say / don't go yet / please stay / he
caught something that I had planted in my eye / an inclined
arch of eyebrow gently raised suggested . . . something /
something sweet / I could almost feel his body's heat. At
last I fumbled in my purse and found a franc / the corpse
next to me snored and turned around / the boy stood still /
as stiff as rock / the thing that I had planted from my eyes
to his / he now returned / it gave me a tiny shock / but not

too much to stop my hand from wandering up / I placed it
like a breath upon the inside of his leg / which felt like
marble angels carved by Donatello / still he held the tray /
and since the beast was snoring deep I opened the servant's
flies and put my hand down deep inside until I found a
large warm penis which couldn't hide / he withdrew a
touch, not much / a trifle scared perhaps of monster waking
and then scenarios of losing needed job / but then I flashed
a pleading look / as if to say it's fun / the old man will not
wake / he caught my look and bravely stayed / and gently
began to squeeze his hips and buttocks / so when I took
him in my mouth it was a gorgeous thrill to do it there with
bastard still snoring in his lair / and then he thrust and
squirted fine silk jets of come and nearly dropped the tray /
the beast next door me waked / but slowly like a drunken
pig / surfacing through mud / the boy retrieved his
shrunken shark / turned on his heel / and made a quick
depart / I meanwhile swallowed fast / then Harry woke /
'Good morning darling' I sweetly slurred / Did you sleep
well? he said like bliss and fastened on my mouth a faggy
kiss / my god I thought he tastes like hell.

STEVE: How decadent darling / how simply fab divine and rare
to gobble the waiter with your husband lying there / how
splendid spiffing whizzo fab and gear / it's the most
enchanting story that ever I did hear / you amaze me, stun,
astound / Oh! Wait till this story goes around / what a plot,
what an amazing scene / let's put it in a play / no one
would believe it anyway / no you can't say those / those
nasty words on stage / you'll have the Tory mothers in a
spitting rage / oh shit, *regardez l'heure* / we simply mustn't
be late / the play starts at a quarter to eight.

HELEN: What are we seeing darling / what's my treat tonight?

STEVE: A play about some filthy soldiers sticking their ends up
some poor tyke.

HELEN: How fabulous / how simply great / I want to see that / I
just can't wait / all those dishy soldiers in the raw with
cocks a-flashing everywhere / how simply shocking / how

awfully bizarre / to train at RADA then at last when you're a
full fledged actor / 'what speech will you do today' / you
turn around and bare your arse / he'll do / a three-year
contract at Waterloo / I love all that / that blood and gore /
to shock us pink and crave for more / do they do it for real
darling / eight times a week?

STEVE: No stupid / or their asses would be sore / they **act** the
buggering / it's an Equity law /

HELEN: Oh darling what a bloody bore / give me realism that's
what I'm paying for!

(*He throws her on sofa and dives on top.*)

(*Light fades and they come up from clinch as* SYBIL *and* LES.)

SCENE 6

(*As they come up from their embrace*)

LES: Was that all right for you?

SYBIL: Yeah – it was great. Was it all right for you?

LES: Yeah – lovely . . . do you enjoy it?

SYBIL: Yeah . . . it was . . . nice . . . did you?

LES: Wo?

SYBIL: Enjoy it!

LES: Yeah – it was handsome.

SYBIL: Les. . .

LES: Wo?

SYBIL: You don't love me no more.

LES: Why say that?

SYBIL: It's a fact.

LES: If I cut off his head, is my love intact?

SYBIL: It shows a willingness, it shows a fact.

LES: A mug an all / a dozy git to put himself right in the shit /
kick out the cunt / cut off his gelt / put him in limbo / set
him loose in the world / stained, dishonoured / a con man
known by all / not a leg to stand on / not even a ball / he

20

won't even show his mug to mum as she sits in shame in the bingo hall.

SYBIL: It don't satisfy me / it chokes me to here (*throat*) to think of that pig out in the strasser dear / stealing more dough / conning some sweet / sucking on her innocent white teat / till he's drained her dry the cunning thief / the bloated vampire / let's extinguish the creep /

LES: You are a one / you are a hag / a right vicious tough old slag / but give me time and then I'll prove I'm twice the bloke you think / kiss me you luscious dolly pink and bouncy / you're a doll / you make me randy.

SYBIL: You're getting back your desperate dan so don't be mean / you know how much I love you so / you're big and strong / ooh your arms are huge / then hold me tight and make me ooze you filthy bastard / touch me doll / stick your hand inside me coat / feel my nipple / hard as rocks / oh sugar I'm just aching for your . . .

LES: Cor blimey, shush / you're putting me off / my mind's ablaze with violent acts inspired by your need for facts / I'll prove I love you / I'll make you see just how wondrous thou art to me / I'll measure my love in deeds so cute / I'll make de Sade go back to school / first of all one night / he comes home / stops the car, alights / my car's just behind and rams him down and pastes him to the side / he needs unpeeling so intense will be my hard caress / in bed one night / he's with his whore / there'll be a little tapping on the door / he, careful as a skunk thinking his trail has left no trace of stink / peeps through the spyhole / and sees me / costumed as a telegram boy / all safe he thinks and opens up / a ten-inch blade dives in his gut / at his squash club / he's had his game / all sweaty in his shower / innocent and tame / in the steam no one sees a furtive me drop a tarantula in his pants / he dries off / dresses and suddenly shrieks / there's something up his Kyber pass and it feels to me like broken glass / 'cause tarantula bite is a vicious sight / or a bomb under the lovers' bed / ready to go off as she or he comes / a neat device so sensitive / that

extra pressure will blow them to shreds / they'll fly / that's
an orgasm that will send them to paradise / gun's too messy
and far too noisy / let's leave that out and choose a poison /
we'll send him a Christmas cake juiced up with cyanide /
lots of sherry to help disguise the bitter acrid taste that
burns his guts / she'll scream in pain / they'll wait as death
starts digging inside their brain / or, excuse me, what's the
time? hydrochloric acid in his eyes / he screams / then in
the dark / a fine needle penetrates his heart / he didn't see
it / so in his dying breath he cannot identify Mr Death / a
minute atomic bomb the size of a pearl / a present in a ring
from his golden girl timed to go off whenever you will / as
the mood takes you ka boom ka blast ke pling! In Africa
from leper colony I extract from a native a deadly smear /
then lace his shaver / one morning you'll hear / Oh I've
scratched myself darling / smile and count down the
minutes my dear / best of all I'll loose some rats whose
fangs have been dipped in a deadly unction / one small bite
and the cunt won't function / longer than it takes to drop
down dead / it also saves disposing of the corpse since the
rats will eat the lot of course / so whatyathink – you make
your choice dove / it's just to show you what I feel **is love!**

SYBIL: Ah darling now I know you care / a little attention
makes a girl all yours / kiss me sweetheart.

LES: Pull off your drawers.

(*Fade out and come up on* STEVE *and* HELEN.)

SCENE 7

STEVE: What are you doing tomorrow darling?

HELEN: Hunting.

STEVE: How absolutely super / marvellous and fabulous – can I
come!

HELEN: Just me and the horse!

STEVE: I bet you're a jolly good rider.

HELEN: You want to practise with me . . . be the horse? . . .

STEVE: What! Can I?

HELEN: Of course. You get down on the carpet . . .
(He does so and she smacks his bum a few times before she starts speech.)

The Chase.

HELEN: The morning hung crisp over the village like a Chanel voile gown or a bouclé ruffle / hunting is so fucking thrilling / if you haven't done it / it's like explaining a fuck to the pope / do you know what I mean? it's the togetherness / the meeting at the morning pub / the stomp of horses and that lovely bloody smell / the preparation, pulling those fucking jodhpurs on / bloody hell they can be tight after a binge the previous night hello Claude and what ho Cecil! There's Jeremiah and Quentin / Jennifer / Vanessa darling you do look fab / that jacket fits you like a glove / the asses of the men look small and pretty bouncing on their steaming steeds / snorting from their sculptured snouts / what a sight / off we go, we shout / the leader of the hounds sounds his horn / they're straining hard 'gainst the curbing leash / a pack of hate / bursting to get free / dying to get that nasty little beast / yoiks and tally ho and onwards we shall go / the bloody fox let loose he scampers out all keenly in the bush / he has a bloody good time / a jolly taste of pure excitement / who doesn't like a smashing race? / The leader sounds the horn the scent's been picked up / dashed good form / heels dig in ribs the horses swing to face the direction of the horn's sweet ring / on we go over hill and dale / watching for the bloody foxy fox's tail / gosh Cynthia's fallen in the muck / bloody bad luck! / over the brook / dash over the stream / my pounding steed's just one with me / it's hard / the saddle chafes / it's tough / my pussy feels delightful though with each successive thrilling dash / it heaves up huge between my thighs / this hot and heaving sweating beast / it tugs my hips / it heaves me on / on to the golden hills of Acheron / I grip him hard / my knees dig in I soar up high / I float / I flow / I'm thrown

into the sky and then thud down / the air is singed in
smells of mud / crushed grass / horse shit and sweat /
mixed up in one divine and bloody mess / we've lorst the
fucker / oh bloody balls the nag's confused / the scent is
lorst / the dogs go searching / now confused / now
whining / now all cross / oh shit and piss! The fucking
league of love the bloody foxes sabotaged the scent! / The
careful thread, the ribbon of fear that leads us on to the
bloody kill / those left-wing bastards jealous as hell / to see
their betters enjoying themselves / threw scent to confuse /
those rotten sods / I'd thrash them black and blue I'd have
them flogged / those dirty, poofy, Marxist, working-class
yobs / wait! Pluto's found the scent again! Oh fab. We're
off! Tarquin bloodies one of their noses! Oh heavens, it's
just raining roses / he's on the ground and Tarquin's ready
to drive his horse into the bugger / Jeremy says nay /
restrains hot Tarquin / they'll come another day! He says /
Oh bravo! Dashing! Super! Wow! I'm going now / look at
meeeeeee! / The day's spun rich in magenta to auburn / the
hounds shriek louder / the scent grows strong / the fox is
tired / my cheeks are red / my eyes are bright / blood will
be shed / oh god it's getting fucking awful thrilling / the
flesh *is* weak but the spirit is willing / my pants have come
galore / and my ass is deliciously bloody sore / we're close /
the fox has gone to ground / we'll find the little beastly
hound / yes! It's trapped down in some gully / horses crash
through the farmer's land / all in a hurry / tear up the
crops / oh dear / we'll pay later never fear / oh fuck! Some
kid's pet cat is torn to shreds in the wake of the
enthusiastic chase / never mind there's plenty more / ah,
we've got him now / I see it caught / it's trapped / its
breath is pounding out in horrible short stabs / its fear
setting each hair on end / the hounds all teeth and smiles as
they go in and sink their fangs into its throat / the blood
was one long jet / just fabulous / I'm sure the fox was
pleased to make his end this way / the fury / the chase / the
ecstasy / the embrace / the leader dismounts / cuts off its

tail / bloodies the kids / oh they were thrilled / oh what a
day / let's have a gin and tonic / whadya say / lovely life /
wouldn't have it any other way /

STEVE: I must say you've made me thirsty / let's have a drink
OK / I enjoyed that / shame about the cat.

HELEN: Ice?

STEVE: Masses (*She mimes handing him the glass.*) I like getting
pissed / like the sound / the crisp crunched feel of bursting
ice / crushed diamonds melting in the acid of your vice / I'll
have a tequila / a frozen glass / grind it into a salt sea bath /
squeezed lemon sharp as a razor / as a spinster's tongue, a
gob of Cointreau adds the dash of fun shake it hard then
pour it out / into your icy salt-licked glass / the first tastes
nice and bitter sweet / grips the tip of your tongue / like the
mouth of a baby on a mother's teat / well have another /
that chases through / warms the furnace / rattles a window
or two / the third one slides along the avenue / well lined
by now and gets to work / a glow appears / your inhibitions
crumble and your fears, they take a gentle tumble / number
four drags from the cupboard your other self / the Jekyll to
your Hyde / watch yourself bloom as four pours blood into
the withered you. No. Five / proves the fact that you're
alive after all / and not a dreary fucking bore / it knocks on
other doors down deep / out come the demons from their
wretched sleep / so pleased at last to be set free / let's have
some fun he! he! he! here comes your past / persecution
mania opens his door / the alcohol prises open a few more /
paranoia, guilt / jealousy and hate / ready to rehearse the
message of agro and bile / you feel good / number six adds
fuel to the fire / there's a party down there raging within /
your best friend now you hate worse than sin / you and
you / piss off you splat / I don't give a shit / accuse and
slag / it's all coming out now / like an acid bath / it unpeels
the old varnish / removes the old scabs / the wounds now
feel fresh, alive and they sting / I throw down number
seven / gis another I sing / insults are woken from
some ancient time / spit out again / some antediluvian

forgotten crime / but I wanna 'nother / I'm having a great time / I'm dragging out the dirty linen and all the grimes / and too much / it dampens the fire / rather than blaze / the one over the edge / the door slams shut in your brain / the demons return to their old domain / Pandora's Box is shut again / you grab another in the hope that you can entice rather than drown but all you've got is slush and sentiment / tears in the eye and howl! Forgive me darling / I didn't mean it / you cry / the party's over / you're left with the mess and your pain / old newspapers lashed by rain / fuck it, I wanna 'nother drink / you've had nine! I don't care no more / it's my second wind / I feel fine / shit it's good / but as the sunset scorches a blazing exit from the skies and just as quickly lays down and dies / so my good feeling pissed off just as fast and left me with an empty glass / gimme – I slurp my number ten / it's late / the light snaps off inside your skull / darkness falls / I feel like hell / and then the next thing then you will espy is the lav staring you in the eye / up come your guts / lurch / past, acids through in one hot stinking steaming stew / your mouth a cesspit of rotting food / it reeks, like shit flows out your head / you just can't wait to get inside your bed.

HELEN: If that's a good time / I'd rather be dead!

(*Fade out.*)

SCENE 8

Scene appears with SYBIL *and* LES *on top of her: same dialogue to begin it as earlier scene.*

LES: Was that all right for you?

SYBIL: Yeah – it was great. Was it all right for you?

LES: Yeah . . . lovely . . . do you enjoy it?

SYBIL: Yeah . . . it was . . . nice . . . did you?

LES: Wo?

SYBIL: Enjoy it!

LES: Yeah – it was handsome!

SYBIL: So with all the thrills and all the spills in the end you're
over the hill / you are no further, no, in the exploit than
when I first discovered my painful plight / you shift your
plates of meat from side to side, plan murder, death,
cyanide. But in the end we watch TV and larf at arse holes
making mugs of all our class / you sit / swill down a jug of
gin / play with your balls / say ''ark at him'! Football and
darts, the mind boggles at the space that runs between your
ears / the working classes ruled always by their peers /
'cause daft you are and thick / that's why you live like
pigs / she, chained to a sink / and my old man / that ponce!
you can't face with your empty bonce / 'cause you're afraid
– his accent frightens you away /

LES: Don't make me laugh / do me a turn / fink his dialogue
will make me squirm / fink a chatter with his nibs will set
old Les a-trembling on his pegs / 'cause he can utter
'olesome tones. It's content, what goes in to make his
bones / it's there the marrow mate! Eff off you stupid
come-pot. Slag-stained hag / you filthy load of ancient slag /
why should I enunciate to him the dirty fink I hate / it's
him that I'll annihilate / without the chatter / with no
threat of tongue wobble banter / like two poofs ready to
tear each other's wigs off. No screaming heebie jeebies no!
When I k'blast him / watch me go!

SYBIL: Yeah tell me another / six months it's been my Les / you
can't make up your mind / like Hamlet in a tizz / you come
all over heavy like a Patton tank / but when it comes to
deeds / your chat is merely wanks / you've lost me Les / I'll
find some geezer new / who will do for me what I do do for
you / some hard determined lad that will not me disgrace /
not lay a single finger on his rotten face! / not volunteer a
bunch of fives to show him your love's alive / let alone / the
murder, death and dark revenge you swore / when you
were in my minge / once there you would swear all / and
like the famous rat / that in escaping from the claws of
some fat cat / falls in a vat of wine / cries out, 'save me!

Save me cat! I'd rather be eaten alive than drown, oh
horror in that vat of wine.' The cat concurs and flips the rat
out on his paws / whereupon seeing himself on steady
floors, rat scarpers to safe hole inside the wall. The cat now
flaming mad to see he'd been so badly had says 'you said I
could eat you rat if I plucked you from out that vat' to
which the rat replied . . . 'you'll say anything when you're
drunk' / that's you all right you punk!

LES: What a turnabout / what a double choke to suffer slagging
from the slut I poke / you think I am not waiting, choosing
well before consigning adenoids to hell / don't make me
piss my pants / don't make me laugh / death takes its time /
it stalks a lonely path. Conditions must be good / the hour
right / don't mess it up and make me rush it / right! I'll
have him sure, I swear I will / but do it all careful like /
now – here's the spiel / I got a plan / now listen to your
Desperate Dan. I'll destroy him with **telepathy**! By my
magic powers I turn on the heat / I concentrate with all my
strength / tune into his wave length and crumble goes his
brain's network, cells and nerve centre go beserk / like
radios jamming enemies' airwaves / my mind will send him
in a rave / he'll freak, twitch and explode when senses he
my vicious probes. I read it in a book how you can work
the spell or spook some geezer into living hell / by
concentration / thinking on his boat / or staring hard at his
mug that's in a phot / fix on his eyes and pour a thousand
evil thoughts inside / he'll cop the message every night like
needles in his brain and burning bright / 'til sickness claim
him like a bride – so much cleaner than cyanide /

SYBIL: Where do you cop that pile of shit / I fink he's doing it
to you, you twit.

SCENE 9

STEVE *and* HELEN.
STEVE: Cigarette?

HELEN: Thanks darling. Nearly killed someone with my car last
    night.
STEVE: Oh really darling. Were you pissed?
HELEN: Couldn't see the bugger.
STEVE: Oh, why was that?
HELEN: He was so damn black.
STEVE: Couldn't you see the whites of his eyes?
HELEN: His back was towards me.
STEVE: I hate the bastards. No no no no no. I won't say that /
    just find them different to us / white is white and brown is
    brown and black is black / you know what I mean? /
    they're fabulous, in their place / in Jamaica I found them
    just ace / a gas / great sense of humour / and move like a
    dream / they're all instinct is what I mean / whereas we
    think / to create and rule / they feel all the time / like
    children and play with their tools / they want before their
    time / they want the taste of power / but their minds are no
    higher than their stomachs / even lower / my God what do
    they put in the shit that they gobble / I can't imagine / it
    makes my knees just wobble / You can't give in to the
    kaffir / to the wog / just because they demand it / my God,
    what would they do to us / they must be trained not to
    rebel / but to use their brain as well / if we gave in to every
    tinpot black / they'd be throwing spears and hurling
    threats / even atomic bombs / yes! / It could come to that /
    they're thick / good natured / more like a dream / but don't
    feel pain / not like us is what I mean / they're tough / more
    like the animals / they kill and chop each other up / life's
    not worth a fig / a string of beads and they'd sell their
    mum / of course we're all brothers under the sun / but I
    hate my fucking brother even if we've got the same mum /
    don't persecute the fuckers / they're all-right blokes /
    there's one down at the club / he takes in the coats / don't
    kill or hurt them / just put them on the bloody boats /
    please Maggie put your money where your mouth is / don't
    be all talk and no fuck / stick up for us – have a little
    pluck. My God she's a handsome woman / I bet the man

who gets inside her pants has a lot to answer for / oh don't look at me like that / we're all the same / there's not a man in England who wouldn't drop his Y-fronts for that dame / still look at the unemployment and sponging in the name of socialism / half of them are on the game / could you touch one love / I mean could you / it's rumoured that they're hung like bloody mules / well it's not such a rumour actually / one day at the club they let in one / the laws that make us do these things / so anyway, in the shower I caught a glimpse of the bugger / I just couldn't believe it darling (*Mimes*) it was simply obscene / it made me feel like a shrimp and you know I'm quite well endowed.

HELEN: (*Fast*) Yes yes darling, of course.

STEVE: He should have it covered up or at least require a yearly licence for it / so I threw down my card at the club office and said / shove that up your jack if you let in any more of that / he's the Prince of Morocco they replied / oh well, I said, that puts a different complexion on the face / of course they have to travel / our royals do it for the trade / they have to shake hands even eat with the bloody spades / they do it for the cash / the foreign office tells them to / you wouldn't catch them with the buggers otherwise / not after work / not in the house / why – they wouldn't get past the dogs who have never seen one in the house /wouldn't know a bloody wog / what! we must preserve what's English / or British if you must, though it's very hard to think of paddy quite like us / there is no place like England / you can't sing there'll always be a Great Britain / it doesn't have the taste / or there'll always be an England . . .

(*Sings, and* HELEN *accompanies. They get through two verses.*) Sorry darling, it brings a tear to my old face whenever I hear that good refrain / let's keep it clean love / let's keep it white / kick out the Pakis, blackies, paddys and kikes / go back to the jungle / Belfast and Israel / don't turn our happy haven into a rancid hell.

SCENE 10

HELEN: We mustn't be late, you mustn't dip your spoon into the cup of hate / it's the first night / the audience will be sheer delight, and I assure you, they will be absolutely white! I'll wear something stunning / I'll just astound / the important thing darling is to make you proud (*She mimes the following.*) I'll wear a fulsome daring Chanel robe / slashed to the thigh / in black cashmere / gathered from the bellies of baby goats / it hugs every line every detail made clear / every vale of my body / every genital contour will amplify itself on my exterior / arms gathered and arranged in gossamer ripples that float in waves / belt by Fiorucci from the skin of snakes that slither round glistening lakes / the gown weighted down at the hem which flares allowing a flash of golden thigh as I climb the stairs / so demure on the outside / such a whore within / fashion is so divine it makes dressing up a sin / a rash display of silver filigree curls round my cheeks / and makes my bum two silver moons that I display for fun / the gown now draws my flesh down from those swelling curves tapering at the thigh / then up it rushes scooping my tits like tasty cherry pies / they softly float inside their silken net like two blancmanges wanting to be ate / a pair of shoes in satin with five-inch heels forged from Venetian glass / opaque and hollow / here small glow worms shine in the dark / my stockings must be silk and finish at the thigh / tops grasped by black suspender belt / like lizard's teeth held tight / my knickers, sheer opaque and thin made from crushed water silk / within, the gusset tiny pleats will hold my special midnight treats / soft and crushy / nice and sweet / my hair is gathered up in waves / is spun and twisted into furls / is plaited, combed and arranged in precious curls / it's modelled on Utrillo's nymph rising from the sea / Sassoon spent many sleepless nights creating this dream for me / my arms, my love will be as long white snakes beneath

transparent tulle / sewn in with chrysoprases and tiny
pearls / I'm ready now darling / let's swirl /
(*Opera music comes on,* STEVE *mimes eating chocolates with*
HELEN, *opera concludes, grand applause which turns into* LES
and SYBIL *slagging each other which then turns back to* STEVE
and HELEN *applauding once more.*)

STEVE: Then after the opera.

HELEN: The supper.

STEVE: Is it at the Savoy?

HELEN: Is it Rules?

STEVE: Kettners is now a hamburger joint.

HELEN: The Caprice is over too.

STEVE: We'll go to the Zanzibar, that will do.

HELEN: My lover holds out my coat / my wrap of pink ermine /
he opens the door / the air smells like wine / that special
time when the evening is yours / gone to bed are the
swine / outside, the porter / the cab is hailed /

STEVE: Taxi!

HELEN: The air crisp and tangy / my lover in tails / expectancy
hangs like some fine perfume / he squeezes my shoulder /
he says /

STEVE: How are you?

HELEN: I'm lovely darling I must reply / we watch the big red
buses go sludging by / heaving their cargoes of workers and
aged.

STEVE: Here's our cab darling.

HELEN: The porter is paid.

STEVE: Great Queen Street please. (*They get in taxi.*) Cigarette?

HELEN: Thank you my sweet / my hands find your prick / I feel
somewhat shy / as cabby in mirror steals sneaky spy the
world is closed to us / wrapped in our love and wealth / I
snuggle up close / your coat is rough / you feel manly and
tough / and smell of musk / your shiny powdered chin and
brilliant teeth / you're a blade all right / you make me weak
at the knees / you sparkle / you thunder / your hat sits just
right / a trilby snapped brim / a Bogart or a Flynn / I like
my man tough / I like to be ruled by an iron fist but a

velvet tool within / I love you opening the doors and
getting the bills / make yourself broke indulging my sins /
being the master / ruling me / a genius in bed / an expert
driving me crazy / weak as a kitten up a tree / let me wait
for your call / let me pine / let me fret / and when the
phone rings / my heart goes pitta-pat / send me an orchid
ply me with perfume / from Givenchy, Chanel and Cardin
as well / say how pretty you look tonight / say how swell / I
can't have enough of that / grab my elbow / squeeze it
tight / guide me darling into the light / like I was helpless /
without my sight / let me blaze like a meteor shower / you
make me feel good / you have the power / I gleam for you /
I sparkle / I'll effervesce display me like a proud conquest /
like a trophy like an animal from the jungle tamed / wild
cat to others / for you love a lamb / you'll be proud / you'll
look suave in your black and white / you devil from hell /
you Lucifer / anti-Christ / you hypnotize me with your
blazing eyes / your adamantine personality / let's go lover /
oh! I must have a pee!

SCENE II

STEVE: We escape to the restaurant / at last some repose / throw
off your coat darling / powder your nose / put on some lip
gloss / I'll splash my toes / hello Giovanni / 'How is M'sieur
and Madame tonight?' / his bright teeth assure us that all is
quite normal and right / all is quite safe / the window's
double barred / 'gainst the dreaded IRA / our table is
ready / how simply hooray / elated wide-eyed / we view the
sight / a river of lords, barons and knights / a stream of
gold, diamonds and pearls / a torrent of lawyers, judges
and earls / a splatter of royalty on top / (*Aside*) (hallo
Charles, hallo Di) just the sauce that lends a perfect flavour
to all / a small royal sprinkling seems to draw from the rest
a flavour that's absolutely the best / Aperitif? Cinzano and
bitter lemon / a crunch of ice / it tastes like heaven / What

would Monsieur and Madame like? Some salmon fumé /
smoked just perfect / its flesh tears like silk / was spawned
in Scotch lakes / hung to be cured by those that know the
secret of salmon / the ones with the nose / to follow
avocado stuffed with prawns / garlic to taste / crushed in a
paste / pear as soft as the bellies of babes / prawns crisp as
ice / champagne Perignon washes all away in its tide / the
mashed hors d'oeuvres / all clean inside / the mouth is pink
and raw once again / to receive like Gargantua its morsels
of fun / what now, oh love decide / steak au poivre or le
boeuf sur le toit, noisette d'agneau or poached turbot / crab
freshly dropped in a boiling scream so its flesh is sunset
pink and taste a dream / filet mignon with oysters crushed
with sauces / that sounds a must / we'll have two of those /
some escargots on the side / they taste so divine / cooked in
sweet herbs and wine / a Mouton Rothschild chilled to a
thaw / wash it down / hmm! Delicious / let's have some
more / I slice the steak / its blood runs free / raw as a
wound / soft as a kiss / I embrace it / I swallow the last
ecstatic piece / it flows like lava into me / a mountain of
spinach and acre of mushroom / we shove it all in and still
there's room / more champagne! It showers away the fish
and the garlic / the slightly acid taste / the burp, the silver
of nausea that starts to grow / from compound of prawns,
salmon, beef, oysters, the sparkly flows / we're fresh again
darling / order / what did you say? More champagne / my
god you're stacking it away / more champagne / dry cold
and wild / what – you've got no more Mouton Rothschild /
well, give us the best, the best that you've got / get fucking
moving you Italian git / no, sorry! What did I say? I was
joking, what / you're my friend / (*Aside*) fucking waiter
pretending he's the bloody end / just 'cause he had Charlie
and Diana to dine / he thinks his piss now tastes like wine /
yes, we'll have some cheese / we'll have some Armontal,
Gruyère, fine herbs and some Brie / it must be dead ripe /
it must ooze gently / just enough / no more / if it's runny
I'll hurl your fucking cheese through the door / I'm joking

you cunt / now don't get sore / more champagne / I said
more / now caviare to finish / taken at the end it's perfect
when you think you can't shove more in your head / a
spoonful of caviare will slither around and find a space
there you hadn't found / more champagne darling? Feeling
all right? Yes! Crêpe Suzette / brandy éclairs / rum babas
and liqueur pears / hmm! That's gurgly / that's rich and
oozy / God it squelches past / my guts are on fire / more
champagne I gasp / I can hardly breathe / give me a cigar /
a brandy / something that doesn't take the remotest inch of
any more space / I couldn't bear to think there's any more
space left / the remotest chink that might house some
morsel / some unexplored delight / that might put the cap
on the perfect night / so now I feel fine / I need a shit / oh
shit, I can't move / I want to be sick / I want to heave up /
be back in a tick / I'll shit and I'll piss and I'll blow the
house down / Ha! Ha! Ha! Oh fuck it's coming up / can
you sick, shit and piss all at once? It must be a record / see
you darling / sorry I'm such a sight /

HELEN: Darling, don't apologize / it's been a wonderful night!

SCENE 12

LES: It's no good / this geezer's got me by the balls / can't seem
to work my little plan / I'm not really a desperate man or
dan / so what he's off with his high-class dame / so what,
for them life's just a game / not like us / working for our
bread / get up / alarm clock near our bed / a bunk up when
we're not too tired from slog / hustling down the highest.
For the cheapest flog / can we afford the trip this year /
we're overdrawn / oh fuck / the kids need more socks /
look what they took for tax this week love / no meat today,
we'll look for scraps / they make a lovely soup / OK /
petrol's up and smokes are dear / it's much cheaper to be a
ginger beer these days it really is / 'cause there's no hope /
no none with kids / in the pub / kicked out at time / 'let's

have your glasses / there's always tomorrow' / but not for
them with clubs / and out all night 'cause they don't have
to graft at break of light / they can lay abed till ten / have
coffee rolls sent in to them / fiddle / screw the state / form
companies and liquidate / they do it legal like, like all of
them / but if we do a straight thieve they shove us in the
pen / at least our thieving's honest / break and enter /
armed robbery / a good old-fashioned thieve / but those
bastards do it legally / lawyers, companies, minutes and
fraud / and end up in the House of Lords / she's right /
whenever I hear his voice I go weak at the knees / it's not
from choice / it's something ingrown like a toenail / the
neverhads have always doffed their hats to those wot have /
it's the voice / the style / the polite smile / with millions at
their beck and call / they can still hold us in thrall / it's like
a pyramid / us at the base / pile of stupid trash / fed by all
that's worst in life / *Daily Mirror* / football, Wimpy bars
and darts / to make sure the workers stay working class /
artless pile of muck / fit only for a piss-up and Fray Bentos
heated up when we get in / and keep your noses down /
here's the boss / here's the police / here's the judge / here's
the royals / ooh! ain't she sweet / what dress will she wear
this week / brain-washed workers waving flags at
coronation dressed in rags / the cost of war is going up / the
bear is on the move again / I do not wish to fight and kill to
satisfy some other pervert's will / when if I take my
vengeance private like / I get ten years / but do it
wholesale / kill a lot in uniform to make it legal / they pin a
medal and make it regal / so my hate's not hot enough / to
shove a knife in this ponce's guts / I'll let him fade out like
the dinosaur / and kick out this bitch my whore.

SCENE 13

SYBIL: Coward like all his kind / why should I fucking care /
when men are two a penny fuck him / snap my fingers, I'll

find some more / they're sitting ducks / all they want to do is . . . need I say it twice / they're all so easy such a bore / a bit of titillation and they're yours / a hard-on makes him soppy as a kid / drooling for his candy / they think of nothing else, and when they're randy / why, it's like taking from a kid his candy / we fuck the bastards / but not quick / just trap them with a tender kiss / sus out the guy and check his bankability / his standing in the world / be careful dear / don't cast your pearls before bankrupt swine / don't fuck for love for fuck's sake / cast your net and wag your tail / they'll soon be slobbering for you / never fails / the child / man-heroes think they claim you as pussy hovers in their dreams / dash that image / or you're just a dustbin for his passion's lust / receptacle for spunk / give him a taste and then withdraw a while / he'll crave for more and more / think your pussy's made of gold and myrrh / he'll write poems to your asshole the pathetic cur / tantalize / don't be too keen / like dope pushers, give the first lot free / hook him first with your sweet sting / then play the game / don't be around when hard-on rings / so then the drug has bit / you're in his blood you won't be so damn free the next time / let him crawl, he'll think you're just the end / you'll be nirvana / a goddess, Aphrodite, perfect divine and rare / to what my love shall I compare thy hair / he'll think he's Shakespeare and go fucking spare / since he thinks that he's found grace / the perfect elusive face / then let him back / be sweet and let the cunt relax once more / even be his little whore / then whack! withdraw!! 'You don't love me any more.' He's hanging on just by his nails / just be unsure / 'I don't know if we're right my dear' / make him grovel, sleepless nights / this bit is very tricky girls and risky too / he may decide he's better without **you** / if he's got strength / one ounce too much / you may lose him and start at square one all again / but chances are, like Pavlov's dogs, the jerk's confused / you now seem, if it works / immortal to the Burke / you're gold-dust, opium, exotic fruit / he's on his knees then kick him in the teeth /

then hold on fast / he's weak / go for the dough / a wife comes next / then in for the kill / house, protection and at last his will / and not the one he leaves / the one that keeps his brains in place / dislodge that and you're made / dangle him a while then snuggle up / be his sweet bride / and then he thinks **he's** conquered in the world the only one that fate for him has squired / he's proud / it's been a chase / an easy game not so laced in danger with that smell of fame / reputation goes up / high-class dame / to trap an animal cunning is necessary but if you trap a lion it's more tough / the going's hard and lonely, but on your wall he makes a smashing trophy / but then it's all the same / beast and human man / they're just big game / you do not get them by being nice / you get them by cunning skill and shrewd device / or else be sweet and honest girl and be well fucked, four kids and end in hell / liberation?? This is it girl!

SCENE 14

They come together for the final dance.

STEVE: I like to dance.

HELEN: I like tea in the Ritz.

STEVE: I like to fly / sipping champagne in the sky.

HELEN: I like to wriggle my hips to the beat in my heart / turn and twist.

STEVE: I like to Fred Astaire and Gene Kelly / I like to lick absinthe off your belly.

HELEN: I like to smell like a wild garden after rain.

STEVE: I like the pleasure I derive after pain. I like holding your ‘waist seeing red rubies glance off your face.

HELEN: Dance under stardust whirling in the sky.

STEVE: Glittering lights / diamonds shattering your eye.

HELEN: Violets, thick carpets and cocktails.

STEVE: Invitations on embossed cards / to rub shoulders with the rich and special.

HELEN: Long fingers bejewelled with art nouveau.

STEVE: Like fireworks burning bright.

HELEN: Pearls and amethysts crushed in white. I like to wake with the sea licking my ears cocooned in silken sheets / my dreams dissolving in the morning dawn so sweet.

STEVE: Like butter melting over hot meat / your ass as round as warm doughnuts.

HELEN: Your cock sliced between my bum.

STEVE: Like a hot dog nestled in a bun / your hair like a soft meadow over the lacy white pillow.

HELEN: The soft knock on the door.

STEVE: The coffee and rolls and first steaming piss.

HELEN: The shower and broiling in a mist.

STEVE: The morning papers white and crisp. Murders and rape . . .

HELEN: Taken with cheese and grapes . . .

STEVE: Stabbings and bombs . . .

HELEN: More coffee my love . . .

STEVE: Earthquakes and deaths . . .

HELEN: Toast and poached eggs . . .

STEVE: Starvation and famine . . .

HELEN: Sausages and gammon.

STEVE: You arise like Venus striding out of the skies.

HELEN: We leave the murder and crime in crunched newspapers never to begrime the spotless lives that are yours and mine.

STEVE: They belong in the other place where people walk in arsenic and hate.

HELEN: Where envy follows greed and becomes the seed that seeks to flower in our pot.

STEVE: No hope of that / we're protected at the top / from our exalted eyrie we float like eagles over the predators below.

HELEN: Who do the pools or any other hype that cons your greedy minds that you may be the one that fortune finds.

STEVE: When the chances are greater that you'll be killed than achieve your fortune by fate's will.

HELEN: So in your beehive metropolis you breathe and hope.

STEVE: Turn on the telly.

HELEN: And go to bed when the weather forecast is read.

STEVE: Your eyes will squint and grow crows' feet staring at the fine print and the lowest price.

HELEN: We have no thought of cost damn it but only what is nice.

STEVE: Your eyes my darling will only read the make and no price tag will ever forbid you to take.

HELEN: You will never arise.

STEVE: No never surmise a better life as long as beer doesn't rise by more than two pence a pint.

HELEN: You'll be all right Jack.

STEVE: Let's go darling it's getting light.

HELEN: Let's watch the dawn arise in its vast magic palace of light.

STEVE: Thanks Giovanni, it's been a wonderful night. Cigarette? . . .

(They both light cigarettes and inhale deeply and as the light fades they age in the results of their debauched lives.)

EAST

*Elegy for the East End
and its energetic waste*

AUTHOR'S NOTE

This play was written to exorcize certain demons struggling
within me to escape. *East* takes place within my personal
memory and experience and is less a biographical text than an
outburst of revolt against the sloth of my youth and a desire to
turn a welter of undirected passion and frustration into a
positive form. I wanted to liberate that time squandered and
sometimes enjoyed into a testament to youth and energy. It is a
scream or a shout of pain. It is revolt. There is no holding back
or reserve in the East End of youth as I remember . . . you
lived for the moment and vitally held it . . . you said what you
thought and did what you felt. If something bothered you, you
let it out as strongly as you could, as if the outburst could curse
and therefore purge whatever it was that caused it. One strutted
and posed down the Lyceum Strand, the Mecca of our world,
performed a series of rituals that let people know who and what
you were, and you would fight to the death to defend that
particular life style that was your own. *East* could be the east
side of any city where the unveneered blast off at each other in
their own compounded argot as if the ordinary language of
polite communication was as dead as the people who uttered it.
I stylized the events further by some cross-fertilization with
Shakespeare and threw in a few classical allusions – this seemed
to help to take it out further into a ritual and yet defined it with
a distinct edge. It still felt like *East* and could not have been
done, I believe, in any other dialect or accent except perhaps
East Side New York. The acting has to be loose and smacking
of danger . . . it must smart and whip out like a fairy's wicked
lash. There is no reserve and therefore no embarrassment. One
critic described it as 'filthy beyond the call of duty' but in fact it
is a loving appreciation of the male and female form. We played
it in three theatres starting at the small Traverse, Edinburgh,
and it was good to hear the kind of laughter that came not only

from the belly but had that ring of familiarity, that sudden explosive yelp of identification, when they laughed hardest, the dirty beasts.

East was first performed at the Traverse Theatre by the London
Theatre Group for the 1975 Edinburgh Festival. The cast was as
follows:

DAD	Barry Stanton
MUM	Robert Longden
SYLV	Anna Nygh
LES	Barry Philips
MIKE	Steven Berkoff
Music	John Prior
Producer	Steven Berkoff

This version of *East* was first performed at the Greenwich
Theatre in July 1976. The cast was as follows:

DAD	Matthew Scurfield
MUM	David Delve
SYLV	Anna Nygh
LES	Barry Philips
MIKE	Steven Berkoff
Music	Neil Hansford
Producer	Steven Berkoff

A new production of *East* was presented at the Regent Theatre
in August 1977.

SCENE I

The stage is bare but for five chairs in a line upstage whereby the cast act as chorus for the events that are spoken, mimed and acted. A piano just offstage creates mood, adds tension and introduces themes. A large screen upstage centre has projected on it a series of real East End images, commenting and reminding us of the actual world just outside the stage. The cast enter and sit on five chairs facing front – piano starts up and they sing 'My Old Man says Follow the Van' – out of order and in canons and descants. It comes suddenly to a stop, MIKE *and* LES *cross upstage to two oblong spots – image of two prisoners photographed for the criminal hall of fame. They pose three times before speaking.*

LES: Donate a snout, Mike?

MIKE: OK I'll bung thee a snout, Les.

MIKE: ⎫
LES: ⎭ Now you know our names.

MIKE: Mike's OK. After the Holy Saint . . . Mike with a hard K. Like a kick-swift . . . not mad about Les.

LES: It's soft, it gooey . . . but choose it I did not . . . in my mother's hot womb did she curse this name on me . . . it's my handle . . . under the soft – it's spiky, under the pillow it's sharp . . . concealed instrument . . . offensive weapon lies waiting.

MIKE: Oh, he doth bestride Commercial Road like a Colossus . . . that's my manor . . . where we two first set our minces on each other . . . and those Irish yobs walk under our huge legs and peep about for dishonourable bother . . . he's my mucker, china or mate.

LES: And he mine since those days at least twelve moons ago when sailing out the Black Raven pub in Whitechapel the selfsame street where blessed Jack did rip and tear in cold thick nights so long ago . . . those muffled screams and slicing flesh no more than sweetest memories of him that went so humble 'bout his nightly graft. Tell how it chanced

47

that we sworn mates were once the deadly poison of each other's eye.

MIKE: He clocked the bird I happened to be fiancéd to, my darling Sylv (of legendary knockers) and I doth take it double strong that this long git in suede and rubber, pimples sprouting forth like buttercups on sunny days from off his greasy boat: that he should dare to lay upon her svelte and tidy form his horror leering jellies . . . so I said to him 'fuck off thou discharge from thy mother's womb before with honed and sweetened razor I do trouble to remove thy balls from thee.'

LES: Oh! Ho! I gushed. You fancied me around the back with boots and chains and knives, behind the super cinema it was then called afore it came a cut-price supermarket (which we have well and truly robbed since then). So round the back we went that night . . . the fog was falling fast, our coat collars were up . . . our breath like dragon's steam did belch forth from our violent mouths . . . while at the selfsame time we uttered uncouth curses, thick with bloody and unholy violence of what we would most like to carve upon each other's skulls . . . the crowd of yobs that formed a ring of yellow faces in the lamplight.

MIKE: Right.

LES: . . . Hungry for the blood of creatures nobler and more daring than themselves.

MIKE: Right.

LES: With dribble down their loathsome mouths they leered and lusted for our broken bottles and cold steel to start the channels gouging in our white and precious cheeks.

MIKE: I thought now fuck this for a laugh.

LES: That's right.

MIKE: So what if sly old Sylv had led me on a touch by showing out to all the lads, provoking hard-ons and gang wars between opposing tribes from Hoxton to Tottenham . . . from Bethnal Green to Hornsey Town from Poplar up to Islington. The clash of steel and crunch of boot on testicle has long disturbed the citizens of those battle-scarred manors and blue-bottles with truncheons hard as iron have had their helmets (and their heads) sometimes removed by rude and lusty lads complete with knuckle-dusters and iron bars nicked from their dads.

LES: Any old iron.

MIKE: Honest and trusty trade upon the streets.

MIKE: ⎫
LES: ⎭ We thought now fuck this for a laugh!

LES: But we could hardly turn back now with five and fifty chinas egging us on there, with shouts of 'come on Les, cut off his cock', and 'punch the fucker's head in.'

MIKE: Or destroy him Mike . . . for fuck's sake don't just stand there . . . nut him in the nose . . . and part his skull from him the greasy turd and yaroo! Yarah! Use your iron . . . put the boot in with shrieks of 'bollocks, slerp! Dog face and fucking hell' . . . 'smash, hit, shithead' . . . 'anoint the cunt with death' one cried (with voice so vehement). Oh Sylv, it was thee, yes, thy gentle voice did sway me finally to deal out pain, then in I went like paste. I flashed my raziory which danced about his face like fireflies, reflecting in the cold wet streets the little yellow gas light, till the sheet of red that splat from out his pipes did dull it . . . just felt that soft thud, thwat, as knife hits flesh . . . You know the feel? It's soft and hard at once and gives you collywobbles with thrilldoms of pure joy.

LES: My pure and angel face, my blessed boat did, on that sacred night receive his homage . . . red did flow – I knew my cheek was gaping open like a flag . . . but never mind, to stop the Tiber, stop myself from kissing death flush on the lips I held it with my hand, held what I could while trickling through my fingers ran my juices sweet as life (*Murmurs of* 'brave Les' . . . 'hard man', *etc*) and then I simply said 'you cunt'. Just that. 'You cunt . . . I'll shit down scorpions of pain upon thee . . . I'll eat you! Get it!!!' My iron found his skull where he had just begun to move but left enough for me to bang and crack a dash, enough bone there to bend and shift a bit . . . split off and

splinter bits in brain . . . his brain . . . splatter . . . the
lads said 'oink and assholes fucking hell! Too far thou'rt
gone and really farted death on him . . . Oh shit . . . swerp
. . . ugh . . . AAAAAARH . . . have it away, before the
law doth mark us for accessory.'

MIKE: So off they flew . . . left me for dead and Les near dying
too in pools of his own blood he lay choked . . . the steel
had bit too deep . . . I felt the silence creeping in . . . and
found myself in an old movie, silent like . . . and flickering
to its end . . . so what? (What's it all about?) Those cunts
have left us, shit in pants (their own) while we slosh round
in guts . . . they watched, were nicely freckled by our gore,
and thought 'Let's scarper now, we had our fun, those
cunts are done . . . let's piss off 'fore the law should stride
with boots hobnailed in woe to grab us in their fat and
gnarled claws.'

LES: We picked ourselves and all our bits from off the deck and
fell into each other's arms . . . with 'What the fuck', and
flashed a quirky red-soaked grin at our daft caper thinking
what a bloody sight . . . we can't jump on the 19 bus in our
condition looking like what they hang up in
Smithfields . . . Those bloody sides of beef (for those of
thee unversed in the geography of our fair state) so we did
crawl and hop . . . stagger and slide 'hold on Mike, nearly
there . . . don't die in Balls Pond Road you berk . . . grip
hard' . . . I only had a pint or two of rosy red in my tired
veins myself . . . the rest I used to paint the town with . . .
would I have strength enough to get there with my new-
found mate, whose brains were peeping out the top of his
broke patch . . . would I not conk out in the street at
Aldgate East (untimely end dear Les of youthful folly) our
mums and dads with bellow, whine and oily tears at our
sad stones . . . we had those visions come and go . . .
they'd tell sad stories of the death of kids who lived not
wisely but too well.

MIKE: We were in love the time we stumbled into the casualty
at Charing Cross. And fell into the arms of white-gloved

saints who sewed a nifty stitch or ten . . . no questions
asked and when John Law did come and mum to visit us
we pleaded we were set upon by those vile cunts from
Tottenham, who picked on us the innocent to venge some
deadly feud from bygone days. The two of us got thick as
tea leaves in a pot that's stewed too long and hatched out in
our white and cosy starched beds a dozen saucy plots of
murders, armed assaults and robbery with harm, bank
raids so neatly planned in dead of night . . . of rape's
delight we'd chat . . . exchange a tale or two of cold-blood
deeds we done in alleys dark as hell and other heinous
escapades too heinous to retell.

MIKE: } Yeah, that's how it happened . . . Yeah, that's it
LES: } . . . she was a bitch, a slag of advanced vile, a pint
of filth . . . but still . . .

SCENE 2

Silent Film Sequence.
Piano.
*A silent film now ensues performed in the staccato, jerky motion of
an old movie. It shows* MIKE *calling on* SYLV *– meeting* MUM *and*
DAD *– going for a night out –* SYLV *is attracted to* LES *– a mock
fight. They are separated and* SYLV's *long monologue comes from it.
The movie sequence reinforces and fills in the events of scene 1.*

SCENE 3

Sylv's long speech . . . She was there.

SYLV: At it they went . . . it weren't half fun at first it weren't
my fault those jesting-jousting lads should want a
tournament of hurt and crunch and blood and shriek . . .
all on my dress it went . . . That's Micky's blood I thought
. . . it seemed to shoot up from something that cracked
. . . I saw him mimicking an oilwell . . . though he'd take

off many things for a laugh this time I did not laugh so
much . . . they fought for me . . . thy blood my royal Mick
wast shed for me and never shall the suds of Persil or Daz
remove that royal emblem from that skirt that many times
you gently lifted in the Essoldo Bethnal Green. I was that
monument of flesh thy wanton hands would smash and
grab, I only clocked the other geezer Mike, and can I help
if my proud tits should draw their leery eyes to feast on
them . . . and now a hate doth sunder our strong love and
never more will my soft thighs be prised apart by his fierce
knees with 'open them thou bitch before I ram a knuckle
sandwich in thy painted boat'. I miss him true in spite of
all and did not wish to see him mashed and broken like a
bloody doll . . . but now the bastard blameth me for all and
seeks vile vengeance on my pretty head . . . which if he
tries will sorely grieve my brothers Bert and George who
will not hesitate to finish off the bits that Les did leave but
all this chat of violence I hate . . . is ultra horrible to me
that thrives on love and tongue-wrenched kisses in the back
of MG Sprites with a 'stop I'm not like that!' . . . Oh just
for now which doth ensure a second date, so hold a morsel
back girls and he'll crave it all the more.

SCENE 4

MIKE *and* LES *commence* 'If You Were the Only Girl in the
World' *which covers the bringing on of the only props – a table and
chairs. On the table are toast, a teapot with steaming tea, a tureen of
baked beans, a packet of margarine – in fact the normal tea-time
scene. They sit around the table and eat. During* DAD's *long speech
he eventually destroys everything on the table in nostalgic fury. The
table and contents become a metaphor for the battle of Cable Street
– his rage becomes monstrous and gargantuan.*

Ma and Pa.
DAD: Mum?

MUM: What?

DAD: What time does *Hawaii Five-O* come on?

MUM: What time does it come on?

DAD: Yeah!

MUM: I don't know dear . . .

DAD: She doesn't know, she watches it every night, and doesn't know.

MUM: (*Reading*) . . . What's a proletariat?

DAD: A geezer who lassoes goats on the Siberian mountains.

MUM: In one word I mean. Six letters.

DAD: *Panorama*'s on first . . . yeah that's worth an eyeful . . . Then we can catch *Ironside*, turn over for *The Saint* and cop the last act of Schoenberg's *Moses and Aaron*.

MUM: Charlton Heston was in that.

DAD: Machinery has taken all the joy out of work . . . the worker asks for more and more money until he breaks down the economy hand in hand with the unions who are communist dominated and make the country ripe for a takeover by the red hordes.

MUM: You haven't paid the licence.

DAD: She's a consumer on the market, that's all, not even a human being but a consumer who's analysed for what she buys and likes by a geezer offering her a questionnaire at the supermarket – makes her feel important . . . I try to educate it but 'tis like pouring wine into the proverbial leaking barrel.

MUM: Suppose they come round.

DAD: Nobody visits us any more.

MUM: They might then you'd go to court and it would be all over the *Hackney Gazette*.

DAD: You don't want to believe all that rubbish about detector vans. That's just to scare you . . . make you think that they're on your tail . . . anyway if anyone knocks on the door we can whip the telly out sharpish like and hide it in the lavatory until they're gone . . . simple . . . say . . . 'There's been a mistake . . . your radar must have been a

53

few degrees out and picked out the hair dryer performing
on her curlers.'

MUM: But anyone can knock on the door . . . you'll have to
start running every time someone knocks.

DAD: When was the last time we had a visitor – especially since
the lift's nearly always broken by those little black bastards
who've been moving in, and who's going to climb twenty-
four floors to see us except the geezer for the Christmas
money – so if anyone knocks on the door it can only be one
of two things – the law inquiring after Mike since they
think he's just mugged some old lady for her purse, or the
TV licence man – in either case I can shove it in the loo!

MUM: Mike doesn't do things like that – I won't have you
uttering such dreadful libels – my son takes after me – you
won't find him taking after you – he is kind to old ladies –
helps them across the road on windy days.

DAD: That was only a subtle jest you hag, thou lump of foul
deformity – untimely ripped from thy mother's womb –
can't you take a flaming dash of humour – that I so
flagrantly waste on you – eh? What then . . . what bleeding
then – thank God he's not a pooftah at least already so soon
– Eh . . . where would you put your face then – if he took
after me the country would rise to its feet – give itself an
almighty shake – and rid itself of all the fleas that are
sucking it dry . . . (*Wistful*) He could have . . . Ozzie*
had the right ideas – put them into uniforms – into the
brown shirts – gave people an identity. Those meetings
were a sight. All them flags. Then, they knew what to do –
take the law into your own hands when you know it makes
sense. That beautiful summer in '38 was it? – When we
marched six abreast to Whitechapel – beautiful it were –
healthy young British men and women – a few wooden
clubs – just in case they got stroppy down there, just the
thoughts of the people letting the nation know it weren't
stomaching any more of it – the drums banging out a

*Oswald Mosley

rhythm in the front and Ozzie marching at our head. We get to Aldgate – if you didn't know it was Aldgate you could smell it – and there were us few loyal English telling the world that England is for us – and those long-nosed gits, those evil-smelling greasy kikes had barricades up – you couldn't even march through England's green and pleasant, the land where Jesus set his foot – they had requisitioned Aldgate and Commercial Road – but our lads, what did they do, not turn back – not be a snivelly turn-coat but let them have it. They soon scuttered back into the tailors' shops stinking of fried fish and dead foreskins – and with a bare fist, a few bits of wood, we broke a skull or two that day – but Hebrew gold had corrupted our fair law and we were outnumbered – what could we do – the oppressed still living there under the Semite claw sweating their balls out in those stinking sweat shops – could only shout 'come on lads' – they had no stomach for it, no strength. It were for them that we had to get through. But we were outnumbered – the Christian Soldiers could not get through this time – not then, and what happened – I'll tell you what happened – by not getting down Commercial Street . . . by not getting down Whitechapel – Alie Street, Commercial Road and Cable Street, Leman Street we opened the floodgates for the rest – the Pandora's bleeding Box opened and the rest of the horrors poured in. That's what happened mate. (*Suddenly*) What's the time?!

MUM: Eight o'clock.

DAD: We've missed *Crossroads*!!?!

(*Blackout.*)

SCENE 5

The table and its contents are splattered to the floor from prior speech. MUM *wipes it up. The five chairs now become a row in a cinema – we see the different films by the piano suggesting the theme from a 'Weepie', a 'Western' and the characters relating to them all*

— MIKE chats up SYLV — DAD goes to the toilet offstage — much vomiting and noise — people change seats — SYLV leaves and MIKE follows — chat is improvised until we see the scene with MIKE and SYLV in 'How the Two Fought for the Possession of'. During it DAD and LES become chorus and mates of MIKE.

SCENE 6

How the Two Fought for the Possession of.

SYLV: She were in ingredients of flesh-pack suavely fresh . . . deodorized and knicker white . . . lip-gleam and teethed . . . shoes thick-wedged with seam running up the back of her leg as if to point the way to tourists pruriently lost . . .

MIKE: She became with me a fun palace in which almighty raging Technicolor and panoramic skin-flicks and three-act dramas would be enacted, a veritable Butlins in one piece of equipment shaped-round-curve and press the button lights flash up . . . there's the bell and off to round one . . . 'Hallo darlin' . . . fancy thee a chat, a meal, a stroll, a drink in the Cock and Bull surrounding a Babycham or two and plethoras of witty verbiage spewing from my gutter mouth . . . with a larf or two . . . they say a laugh doth provide the key to open Pandora's Box of dirty tricks.

SYLV: Piss off thou lump. Though hast no style for me get lost . . . too old . . . too young . . . too slow . . . I'm too trim for thee and move like what you dream about (on good nights) I'm sheer unadultered pure filth each square inch a raincoat's fantasy – all there swelled full – I am the vision in your head – the fire you use to stoke your old wife's familiar stoves (you know what I mean) . . . sag not – pink tipped, tight box, plumbing perfect – switches on and off to the right touch . . . not thy thick-fingered labourer's paws thou slob and street-corner embellishment . . . thou pin-table musician . . . thy flesh would ne'er move – would shrink under my glare – so try.

MIKE: Tasty verily – so thou, bitch, seeks to distress my johnny
    tool with psychological war, humiliating it into surrender-
    shrink . . . I could mash thee into and ooze with my
    personality-plus once turned on . . . Full blast . . . dance
    thee to death and once touched, one clawful of lust-
    fingered-spread-squeeze resist that hot-bitch how many up
    and downs have thee got stacked away merrily depreciating
    unless thou dost invest wisely and shed a few on the market
    sample-like be greedy not and unleash a few.

SYLV: I wrap my goodies up for special heroes crashing thigh-
    clutched Harleys and angels of hell, leather skinned,
    tattooed in violent histories of battles too screaming
    delirious for verbal-mere-pub-splatter . . . loose-tongued
    garbage in the vile (look-for-the-red-door) with a blah blah
    . . . you are out-classed. You. You.

MIKE: I'll descend on thee like a moon probe, thou planet of
    delights fleshy . . . advance my antennae, vibrating back to
    the lust-computerizing cells the sanguine goodies that do lie
    unmined . . . I'll chart thy surfaces until thou criest from
    within thy depths, subterranean and murky and foetid
    swamps, 'Mike oh Mike', fluting gurgled falsettos from thy
    lips of coral, 'What dost thou dooo! . . .' I'll rip off my
    clothes and gaberdine and make thee view the sight that
    sent Penelope mad and wait ten years for that . . . the girth
    of a Cyclops to stun to stab, screams like Attila, growls,
    snarls, froths, foams and speaks to you in a thousand ways.
    The length of an ass, the stamina of a Greek, the form of
    Michelangelo's David, the strength of a Westminster oak,
    as solid as a rock, as tricky as a fox, as lithe as a snake, as
    delicate as a rose, the speed of a panther, reflexes match the
    piston power of the Flying Scotsman, as hot as hell – as the
    forge whereby the shoes are beaten for the horses that drag
    the sun round the earth each day, as pretty as Paris, its
    helmet matches the battering ram that felled the walls of
    Troy, its shape like the crest of Achilles, *balls* like the great
    cannon that Pompeii used to subdue the barbarian, as
    spherical as the mighty shield of Ulysses, as rich in goodies

as the Tiber bursting its banks, its juices as sweet as the
honey from the little wasps of Lesbos that only live a day,
as sweet as the dripping that mum puts on the Sunday
joint, and with this magic sceptre that laser-like splits and
cracks through walls, I'll fill you full till thou'll not feel one
shred of space not occupied by flesh-blood-splech-filled-
slurp . . . tongue tied, lava flow-flesh eat. Where thy arse
rises creamily mocking Bertorelli's ice-cream, the trembling
domes of the mosques of Omar bounce, weave, bob, groan
and whine, Oh, you're the spring time after fierce winter
. . . buds sprout . . . opening . . . little whisper in the
hawthorn . . . Oh! I thought thy planet shook then, caught
thee then a word did it . . . Pandora's Box teases open,
does it with a yes . . . yes . . . yes . . . No! No!
YESYESYESYESYESYESYESYESYESYESYES . . .
(*Blackout.*)

SCENE 7

Sylv's Longing Speech.

SYLV: I for once would like to be a fella, unwholesome both in
deed and word and lounge around one leg cocked up and
car keys tinkling on my pinky. Give a kick* at talent
strolling and impale them with an impertinent and fixed
stare . . . hand in Levi-Strauss and teeth grinding, and that
super unworrisome flesh that toys between your thighs,
that we must genuflect and kneel to, that we are beaten
across the skull with. Wish I could cruise around and pull
those tarts and slags whose hearts would break as he swiftly
chews us up and spits us out again . . . the almighty boot!
Nay, not fair that those pricks get all the fun – with their
big raucous voices and one dozen weekly fucks . . . cave
mouths, shout, burp and Guinness soaked . . . If I dare do
that . . . 'What an old scrubber-slag-head' utter their fast

*eye up

and vicious lips . . . so I'd like to be a fella. Strolling down
the front with the lads and making minute and limited wars
with knife-worn splatter and invective splurge. And not
have the emblem of his scummy lust to Persil out with
hectic scrub . . . just my johnny tool to keep from harm
and out of mischief . . . my snarling beasty to water and
feed from time to time to rotten time . . . to dip my wick
into any old dark and hot with no conscience or love groan
. . . doth he possess the plague in gangrened bliss to donate
to me and not give a shit. I am snarled beneath his bristly
glass-edged jaw, beneath a moving sack of leer and hard
and be a waste-bin for his excessives and embellishments
and No . . . no . . . not tonight my friend, a dangerous
time is here in case your tadpoles start a forest fire in my
oven or even just a bun . . . you won't will you? . . . you
will be careful (Yes!) . . . you won't . . . not inside (No!)
Not tonight . . . ('Doth thou not love me then') he quests
('nor feel my intense pain, then see me not again, for you
must sacrifice thy altar of lust-pink and pornographia to my
tempered sullen and purple swollen flesh.') Oh Micky!
Micky! Wait until tomorrow. ('Tomorrow I may be dead,'
he chants in dirge of minor key . . . 'by then my softly
flesh may lie in shreds and curling on the streets a victim of
nuclear aggro from the powers that deal out death on
wholesale scale and liquidize your little Mick to tar, and
what was once a silken mass of moving ecstasy
programmed by filthy raunchy lust lay now a charred and
bitter heap.') Oh who can put it back again those swivel
hips/ball-bearing joints flicker spine and tongue like a
praying mantis . . . ('so listen', he adds 'dunk-head and
splatter-pull . . . seize the time before time doth seize thee
. . . you of the intricate wrist and juice imbiber from the
holy North and South.' He sprach . . . 'Give me all now or
"it" may with my balls explose, such things are known
when passion's smarting angels are defied and I may die in
loathsome sickness here upon this plastic and Formica
divan (mum and dad meanwhile in deathly lock of wrath

from heavy bingo economic loss) . . .') So wrench open
deflower unpeel, unzip . . . pull off . . . tear round knee
tights stuck . . . get your shoes off . . . Ow. Knickers
(*caught on heel*) . . . OOOh, zip hurts . . . dive in and out
. . . more a whip in, like a visit – quick, can't stay just
sheltering from the rain – cup o'tea hot and fast . . . hot
plunge-squirge and sklenge mixed for a brief 'hallo'. A rash
of oohs and aaaahs quiver and hummmmmmy . . . mmm
. . . then hot and flushy he climbs off (come in number
four) and my tears those holy relics of young love tracing
mortal paths to Elysium down my cheeks . . . while the
'he' with fag choke and smoke . . . tooth-grin-zip-up . . .
me lying looking at the future flashing across the ceiling.
He, flashing his comb through his barnet and reddened
cheeks blood soaked (like a saucy cherub, so lovable
sometimes you know how boys have this lovely thing about
them, some little-boy habit that makes them adorable,
crushable-eatable-sweetable-dolly cuddly though sometimes
you could kill them) and me lying there a pile of satiate
bone and floppy tits flesh-pinched and crack-full of his slop
containing God only knows what other infernos but
thought I tasted something very strange on his straining
dangle which he is wont to offer to me sacrificial like . . .
Oh let me be a bloke and sit back curseless, nor forever
join the queue of curlered birds outside the loo for dire-
emergency . . . do we piss more than men or something
. . . nor break my heels in escalators and flash my ass,
ascending stairs, to the vile multitude who fantasize me in
their quick sex-lustred movies in which I am cast as the
queen of slut and yield . . . let me be a bloke and wear
trousers stuffed and have pectorals instead of boobs,
abdominal and latissimus-dorsi, a web of knotted muscular
armature to whip my angered fist into the flesh-pain of
sprach-offenders who dare to cast on me their leery
cautious minces . . . stab them with fear and have a dozen
flesh-hot weekly . . . sleep well and mum fussed, breakfast
shoved, 'who's been a naughty boy then', to this pasty

wreck of skin and bone gasping in his bed skiving work through riotous folly, bloodlet assault and all night bang and 'our lad's a lad, and sown his wild then has he and did you cut yourself a slice' . . . while 'get yourself to the office Sylv or you'll be late,' and the sack in its bed is parlering for another cup of rosy. He's lying in bed whiles I'm on the Underground getting goosed in the rush hour between Mile End and Tottenham Court Road by some creepy asshole with dandruff, a wife and three accidental kids and who's probably in the accounts department . . . most perverts come from there.

SCENE 8

LES *comes down downstage and mimes office scene, says* 'Miss Smith would you please take this to the accounts department.' *As she complies he gooses her and shrieks with maniacal joy thus fulfilling the prophecy in her last speech. His leaping up and down dissolves into a seaside scene –* MIKE *bouncing a ball.* SYLV *skipping, etc.* DAD *and* MUM *enter.*

DAD: Years ago things were good, you got value out of your money, a dollar was five bob, a summer's day was hot and sunny like a summer's day, you weren't short changed, you got your full twelve hours' worth, then we'd take the train from Liverpool Street to Leigh-on-Sea and walk to Southend, go to the Kursaal Amusements . . .
(*On the words* 'Kursaal Amusements' *the cast become bumper cars – roller coasters. The ghost train.* 'I've Got a Lovely Bunch of Coconuts' *is sung – What the Butler Saw. Ice-cream sellers. The Carousel. Swimming in the sea.* MUM *gets out the sandwiches and Tizer –* SYLV *takes a photo, then so does* MIKE. *The scene should be improvised and the mime accurate and clear. The piano reinforces all the vignettes. It leaves* LES *alone on stage at the end of the last photograph. The scenes of fun at Southend delicately indicating* LES's *sense of isolation.*)

61

SCENE 9

Les's Tale of Woe when he did Sup on Porridge.

LES: (*Start slow pianissimo and build*) I was lonely, you know
what I mean. Just lonesome basically I think, like is one
born that way, I always felt lonely as if it was something
like a habit, or the colour of your hair . . . like even a bit of
clobbering now and then, the taste of pain and blood, was
like an act of love to me: so when two nifty lads went
round the back to bundle, it could be like your bird that
you pulled round for stand-up charvers. And sometimes
you would pull ('cause you were lonely basically) anything
that came along . . . so she looked at me, I crossed the road
and gave it a bit of chat, just some bird of tender years or
jail bait if you like. Maybe fourteen or fifteen. I said meet
me after work, she said OK why not, with a tiny giggle and
freckles leaping all over the place, and I was working in
this dump, impersonating Frankenstein, a place where you
stood round pretending to be busy – one of those stores
where you'd try to con people into buying what they didn't
want, a grimy little men's wear shop, not a geary boutique
but full of rotten little grotty striped ties and collar studs,
('don't forget to dust the cuff-links Les. Straighten out the
ties Les') where you stood around dying and acquiring bad
breath, pop eyed for a pathetic wet customer to bleed.
Horrible beige pullovers bought by the wives of Irish
navvie's who'd come back to change it half a dozen times
'cause we always bunged them whatever size we had in
stock ('don't take a swap Les, get their gelt, they can
always change it') . . . incredibly crummy blazers hanging
in a rack like dead fish on parade, shirts with drab little
collars with a million pins, in two-tone checks that
hangmen and clerks would buy with shit-coloured ties to go
with them . . . and maybe a cardigan in maroon . . . this
month's colour . . . the wives trotting round the mirror
anxious for their fifty bob, the manager's loathsome mask
that he wears for a face creases like Fu Manchu. 'A nice tie

to go with it sir? How are you fixed for shirts . . .
Okayeee?' His eyes look like two gobs of phlegm, he sits in
the back room where they kept those fucking horrible Y-
front pants that make you look like a rupture case – he'd
sit there so greasy you could fry him – in that dirty little
back room he'd be watching – having his crummy little tea
break . . . ''ere Les, go get us a cake will ya son . . . a
chocolate éclair or something' . . . 4.15 His looked-
forward-to tea break in a day that poured down boredom
like yellow piss . . . his frog's eyes bulging in case you
didn't sell the shop-soiled crew neck six sizes too big to
some innocent black cunt. 'Yeah it fits you beeauutiful!
Lovely shade, it goes with anything' . . . he spits as he
rushes out of the back room like a great huge dirty spider
with bits of éclair sticking to his revolting fat lips . . .
'Fuck me! Les we got to top yesterday's figure,' he
squelched from the side of the mouth, a hiss like a rat's fart
. . . but the black is confused by being surrounded by faces
the colour of plague victims, all the retchy salesmen with
bent knees and worn-out grins. Yellow-teethed vultures
whose eyes vaguely send out a couple more volts every time
the shop door opens. 'Only take thirty minutes for lunch
on Saturday – busy day for shirts' . . . some slag says 'that
one in the window', 'Oh show me which one you mean
love', any excuse to escape and breathe some fresh air
fumes from the lorries and buses belching past which is as
fresh as a Scottish loch compared to the smell in the shop
of rotten cancered flesh laced by a few farts when everyone
scatters. 'Oh fuck, Harry's farted again' . . . chortle-burp
. . . all the macabre and twisted figures of humanity oozed
through that deceased testament to Beau Brummel, that
charnel house of gaberdine and worsted hell . . . the living
corpses – slack mouths and brains waiting for 6 p.m. or
death, one of the two or both – hands in pockets playing
with anything that reminded them that they had a tiny dot
of feeling left – standing there like it was a way of life. I
was thinking of that bird which was making me very

anxious about the Hickory-Dickory and impatient to act out a few skin scenarios floating around in my skull. At 6 p.m. the morgue closed for the night. I'd check the gelt I half-inched, not a bad day a few ties wrapped round my waist – given a dozen pairs of socks to my mate and watch Mr Greasy with fag hanging out of his perpetual mouth check his cash. The cunt never found out 'cause his brains were soaked in grease, his lungs in cancer and phlegm and his jacket in dandruff . . . so I escaped from that place wondering how I might burn it to the ground with all of them frying in the manager's grease. I saw her as planned and she was waiting for me like she said she would, and that had kept me going for the day – had stopped me from going insane, the idea of the two of us hacking away at each other's goodies – that was something real, alive . . . that would give a bit of meaning to my life – us two locked away in a little cosy place, where I could crawl out of my skin and get into hers, sweat, pant and shriek – so she was standing there, happy like it was Xmas and she said yes and I took her back to my pad all freckling and giggling and then she delivers her history in a funny Irish – how she's pissed off at home with a mad Irish dad who beats her and whiles I pacify her with a quick, svelte and heroic in and out, she says could she stay with me since she's bound to be clobbered by her paddy daddy for being so late. I demur to the riotous demand with full awareness of the Law's nastiness to the souls who taste young flesh and instruct her to the bus to take her back to evil Kilburn. Just one hour later I was in the middle of some shrewd interpretations of the theory of relativity and just getting into the quantum theory and boggling how light would take 200 billion years to get round the universe, when bang bang at the door and two thick-eared brainless cops come yobbing in. Dressed in the kind of clobber I'd been flogging all day, scaring the shit out of me and the cats – the mad Irish had gone to the johnny law with some mad tale of rape and kidnap to avoid chastisement at the hands

of dirt-head dad. Grabbing me in their thick fingers (not
made for Chopin's 'Etudes') they call me 'dirty bastard'
and other unflattering epithets while breathing their foul
vomit breath in my face, 'I'll kill thee' I spray (hair on end)
'not now, not tomorrow but one day I'll eat your eyeballs,
I'll bathe you in acid, I'll stab your fat guts with ice picks
when lying in your bed beer-soaked bloated, thick with
haze and swill like drunken pigs, I'll stab and thrust until
your tripe explodes,' which doubtless did not go down very
well, since they pounded all manner of horny fist into my
soft and sweet flesh . . . those harbingers of death . . .
those wholesale legal sadists . . . those lawmen did believe
the slag, which got her off the hook, and rendered carte of
blanche to them for fun and thump, and poor old Les
before a graven magistrate is dragged who chides and
moralizes 'bout snatch too young for me while thinking of
his handicap in bed and golf and house in Esher Surrey, his
furtive weekly whore and sessions of paid lash, looking
down at me from dizzy heights he says he would be lenient
and I reply from the bottom of my black and lying soul, of
'heartfelt sorrow', and 'never again', and then he said,
'three years I curse on thee' and as he did I heard my
mouth reply that he would die a death in fire so slow he'd
rather be eaten alive by ants while bathed in honey . . . 'I'll
kill you a thousand times over' . . . I shouted to the world
at large and as they dragged me screaming down some cold
stone corridor my shouts sent curses ripping through his
skull, and now my curse comes true.

MIKE: So how did you kill him Les?

LES: I doubt if I should let on now, lest hungry ears attend, you
do not know whose flappy lugs may bring a fate too
horrible for verbs upon my lovely head. But content
yourself I did.

MIKE: There's no one here but us and our rabid desires.

LES: I think I hear the beating of a hundred hearts.

MIKE: Only us and our imaginations, as foul as Vulcan's stithy.

LES: What are those sighs and murmurs, soft groans?

MIKE: The punters who paid for a seat to witness thy foul and cruel beauty, that will haunt them in their dreams.

LES: Do you mean we're in a play?

MIKE: Something of that kind.

LES: I am not, even if you may be.

MIKE: You mean to say . . .

LES: Exactly, you sussed it true, I am no player who struts and frets his hour upon the stage and then is heard no more.

MIKE: You guessed aright, I am that merry wanderer of the night.

LES: You've made a time slip into the wrong play.

MIKE: I am caught in a time–space trajectory.

LES: Can you see me . . . I can only just see you.

MIKE: Yes, but you're fading fast. What's happening?

LES: Think you've hooked on to an errant radio wave from C56, your own waves are sacrificing themselves to its force until your anti-matter coalesces.

MIKE: Fuck! What can I do . . .

LES: Nothing, just go with it. I'll tell your mum and Sylv.

MIKE: OK. See ya around sometime . . . I've lost you now . . . can you hear me? . . .

LES: Only just . . . see ya . . .

(*The whole cast become involved in the latter part of the scene . . . floating slowly in space until* MUM *settles down with legs comfortably sprawled over* DAD *on two chairs stage left. The three other actors face offstage and* MUM *is lit in her own space. She takes out a cigarette and commences her speech.*)

SCENE 10

Mum's Point of View.
DAD *is sleeping.*

MUM: Sometimes I get gorged in my throat I see him sleeping – lump sweaty, beer gutted – farty – no hope – thick brained and me the other half of nothing fed with electric media swill – consumer me – *Hawaii Five-O – Z Cars –*

*Coronation Street – Beat the Clock – University Challenge –
Sunday Night at the London Palladium – On the Buses – Play of
the Month – Play of the Week – Watch With Mother* – tea, fags –
light and bitter – ha! ha! and ho! ho! Bingo – Eyes down –
clickety click – *What the Papers Say* – Reg Varney – *The Golden
Shot* – Live Letters – Tits – Green Shield Stamps (*Pause.*)
Hallo dear how are you? Turn over shut up and let me sleep –
fart belch the music of the spheres. Got a clean shirt? Who's
running at Epsom? 500 more troops being flown in tonight –
the Pill is safe – abortions rise – I would like to practise today –
Tippett's 'Sonata number 3'; six hours of it, I must be ready for
my BBC recital on Wednesday – then I may pair it with
Mozart's 'Concerto in C' – Terry Riley, mind you, needs
dextrous finger work – I'll leave that for now and pick up my
percolator at the Green Shield shop – Wall's pork sausages for
supper and Fray Bentos peas – McDougall's flour for a smooth
pastry – do I smell? Does my mouth taste like an ashtray? Will
my lover meet me after I play Brünnhilde in the Ring at the
stage door of Covent Garden and buy me filet mignon in Rules
Café or the Savoy? Will we drink champagne and discuss our
next production of Verdi's *Otello*? He's longing to play Otello –
but wants Bernstein to direct – I'd be happy with Visconti
really – Maria is coming to tea – must get some Lyons jam tarts
– I met Hemingway in the Brasserie Lipp today, he said my
poetry soars to heaven. Come and have some wine with
Gertrude, there will be some very nice people there.

FATHER: (*Waking up*) Shut your gob. Can't ya let me bleeding
    sleep?
    (*Blackout.*)

SCENE II

Mike and Les.

MIKE: How's Doris – the imbiber of thy resin with her holy
    North and South?

LES: All right.

MIKE: Seeing her tonight?

LES: No!

MIKE: Oh! What happened?

LES: Loaded off her box to other's greedy paws.

MIKE: Almighty slag.

LES: I told her to get to a nunnery, in other words piss off.

MIKE: I thought you were a bit touchy.

(*Pause.*)

LES: I was on the bus today – I jumped on the 38 goin' towards
Balls Pond Road, the one that goes to Leyton – I mounted
at Holborn – just been to the British Museum to look at
the Elgin Marbles which were double fair but too big to
half-inch and I was standing, since there were no seats, in
the recess where the clippie normally stands – you know
when it's quiet she stands there chattin' and making thin
jokes to the seats that face each other, having a quiet fart as
the bus makes its last journey down Piccadilly up
Shaftesbury Avenue you know past *Jesus Christ* – up
Charing Cross passed that cinema showing *I was A Go Go
Dancer in a Saigon Brothel* – spins around the Centre Point
Synagogue and skates down Holborn – up Mount Pleasant
Post Office where the spade post office workers are skiving
in the betting shop, past the Angel where Joe Lyons used
to be, where one's mum supped famous cups of rosy amidst
merry parlance, now it's boarded up, down Essex Road,
past Collins Music Hall, now a rotten wood yard, past
Alfredo's café, you know where one gets great toasted liver
sandwiches, streaks passed the ABC, now a shitty bingo
hall to the end of Essex Road, now a casbah full of
shishkebab.

MIKE: A veritable tour of our golden city.

LES: Shall I continue?

MIKE: Pray do.

LES: Anyway I jumped on at Holborn and stood in that recess
where the clippie stands, when I saw the most awful
cracker. A right darlin' – I stood there clocking it, wanting

her to get the message, dulcet filthed, she was blonde with medium-length hair, dyed straw but soft and straight and her legs were phenomenal. She had this short skirt on – and it had tucked gently between her legs in case she flashed her magic snare to some snatch bandit like me – and faces jumped on and off never quite hiding my angel from me but those legs with well-carved calves poured into some very high thick-wedged shoes. She was a darlin' – I could have breakfasted out of her knickers so sweetly pure she was – I could have drunk the golden nectar from that fountain, I could have loved her – wrapped her legs round my throat, her bright arse trembling in my hands. Divine she was and wore dark glasses but not so dark I couldn't see that finest glint as she occasionally clocked me vardering her like an ogre with a hard-on, ready to leap across the bus and say darlin' climb aboard this, but she was almost too perfect. I stood all the way – unable to leave, like a sentinel at the post and my lover was there – and I thought, Mike, I thought of Doris and I thought of all the fat scrubbers I get with soggy tits – I thought of all those dirty scrubbers and how, just once in my life I'd like to walk down the street with that. Why don't we chat up classy snatch? Why is it that we pull slags? We pull what we think we are Mike – it tumbled then – it dropped – the dirty penny – that we get what we ARE. What we think we are, so when we have a right and merry laugh with some unsavoury bunk-up or gang bang behind the Essoldo we are doing it to ourselves. We are giving ourselves what we deserve. It came to me then – here it was, the most delectable snatch in the world REAL with those INCREDIBLE pins and CLEAN – and then she stirred just ever so little it was but she knew I was lapping it up – and she uncrossed her legs to get up. She was going but maybe my wires got through to her and she thought why not give that geezer – he's not a bad looking bloke – a flash and as she uncrossed her DIVINE THIGHS I swivelled my sockets up there and some creep moved right in front of

her but I just caught the slightest glimpse of heaven – the
clouds passed over the sun but it reappeared again – she
stood up on the platform waiting to leap off at Farringdon
Road with that thin skirt on – a thin black cotton skirt –
God she must have known that the sun pours through that
skirt – no slip, just her AMAZING FUCKING FORM.
Up to the ARSE. Like she was naked, standing there
waiting for the bus to stop at Mount Pleasant where she
jumped off – and I wanted to jump off Mike – I wanted to
get off the bus and run after her – but what could I say –
she strode down the street – strong on those DELIRIOUS
PEGS with those nasty post office workers leering her
beautiful form with their dim and faded jellies and I
couldn't get off the bus – I didn't have the guts – I didn't
know what to say to her Mike! What words could my gob
sprach?! And then I saw her cross into Clerkenwell Road
when she disappeared.

MIKE: 38 bus! You want to get yourself a motorbike.

SCENE 12

The two lads wander upstage to a special spot – MIKE *turns* LES
into a motorbike and jumps on his back using LES's *arms as handle-
bars. The two clearly create the sound of a motorbike revving up and
changing gear during the scene. The strength of the engine and the
movement as it careers round corners should be apparent.*

Oh for Adventures.

MIKE:
    I'm a Harley Davidson with ape-hangers
    Or maybe a chopper, made to measure to fit me
    A built-up Triumph 1000 cc. A Yamaha or a Suzuki maybe,
    Yeah, but who wouldn't mind a Vincent HRD!

LES: With apes?

MIKE: No – not on your Vincent HRD it's too classy, not on
    that – that's sacrilege. At a 150 a ton and a half of sublime

speed tearing gut winded flailing flesh pulled – your glasses
stabbing in your eyes – ice ripping off your face – the
vibrations pulsating through each square inch of skin
between your thighs power lies – at 2000 cc my throttle-
twist grip lightly, oh so delicately held – not too much rev!
We skate! We fly! Between my thighs I grip her tight – she
won't budge – won't skid – road clears for us – it opens up
like a river – the cars farting families in VWs and Fords,
with dogs and kids smearing up the rear windows and
granny spouting they ought to be exterminated – standing
still they seem – I streak past those ponces and hairdressers
in Minis, Sprites, MGs, menswear salesmen in green
Cortinas, or ancient Cadillacs driven by ageing movie stars
cruising for rough trade and liking the leather-loin boys
with long records of glorious GBH tattooed on the helmets
of their cocks. I slow down to 150 miles an hour and chat it
up – her face is hanging off her skull, she sees what grows
between my knees and creams her jeans. 'Stop James,' she
says and we split – down to Joe's café at the intersection
where the M1 sludges reluctantly off into Luton, I mean
who wouldn't be – there behind the café behind the
pantechnicons and articulated lorries I ram it into her
ancient North and South. 'Take out your teeth you old
slag,' and I leave her with a happy grin on her toothless
retchy boat. James carries her off with a nod suggesting
here we go again – never mind it's all in a day's work –
start up my beauty once more nice and gently – open up
the throttle very slightly, no more than an eighth, depress
the kick starter – now I feel it coming to life – warming,
buzzing down there it's loving it – she's randy now. Now
kick the starter in the jacksie – smash the brute down –
ZAPP! We're off – she rises – she moves like it had teeth –
like it was hungry – like it KNEW where to go and she
sings to me everything's checked, everything's beautiful all
checked.

LES:	MIKE:
Headlamp?	Check
Tail-lamp?	Check
Pilot bell?	Check
Carburettor?	Check
Alter-jet needle?	Right
Position?	Right
Float chamber?	Right
Tickler?	Right
Sparking plugs?	Check
Clean out?	Right
Oil your lubricator?	Lovely
Remove dynamo?	Lovely
Inspect brush gear?	Lovely
Keep it jacked up?	Lovely
Ready to start?	Lovely
How's your oil?	Lovely
Stand astride	Yeah!
Turn on the taps	Yeah!
Open your throttle	Yeah!

Song

    I am a Harley Davidson
    I am a Harley Davidson
    I am a Vincent HRD
    I am a Vincent HRD
    I fly like a king
    I kill like a sting
    I smash down the road
    I crush those other fuckers
    Those Hell's Angels like toads

MIKE: ⎫
          ⎬ (*Sing* 'Underneath the Arches'.)
LES: ⎭

    (*The two boys separate and become a raging duet enacting their
    passion for the bike. At the end of the song which is screamed
    out they go into* 'Underneath the Arches', *sung delicately,*

*which covers the next dining scene and the table is brought on
in the condition it went off –* DAD *repeating the first part of the
speech again.*)

SCENE 13

Dad's Soliloquy for Happier Days.

DAD: Years ago things were good, you got value out of your
money, a dollar was five bob, a summer's day was hot and
sunny like a summer's day – you weren't short changed,
you got your full twelve hours worth, then we take the
train from Liverpool Street to Leigh-on-Sea and walk to
Southend, go to the Kursaal Amusements. It was fun then.
On Sunday you'd get cockles and whelks from Tubby
Isaacs on the corner of Goulston Street, eat them outside
and walk down Wentworth Street to the station past the
warehouses – 'Got the sandwiches mum?' – 'Yeah – all
packed' – bottle of Tizer – your Mike only five then before
he saw the inside of a detention centre or Borstal. That was
his bad environment that was – all those dirty rough-
necked Irish bog-diggers whose kids set him up to snatch
handbags – never got it from me . . . Never mind. Then
we jump on the train – mum and Ethel, her sister – she
don't half gas but what a larf . . .

MIKE: Who's Ethel?

DAD: You know. Big fat Ethel, covered in warts. No disrespect
but she looked like a tree trunk coming down the road.

LES: She suffered from tree trunk legs.

DAD: Elephantiasis is the correct medical name. I looked it up.
Here, young Mike was a terror even then. Unscrewing the
light bulbs and chucking them out of the window.

MIKE: (*Proud*) I did that?

DAD: Of course you did, all the way down to Southend. (*Bop
bop bopbop*)

MIKE: I never.

DAD: You did, five years old you were. You stood on my
shoulders! I still have the bill in the sideboard from Eastern
Region. They banned us in the end . . . we'd go up to the
station and say five please . . . they'd say piss off out of it!
. . . no more light bulbs! You remember, we became
known as no more light bulbs! Weren't we, mum?

MUM: (*Distant manner*) What? . . .

DAD: Never mind. The East End was rough then, still half
down, and the kids would catch the water skaters from
those septic rancid tanks near the bomb sites. All the abes
used to sit outside in Anthony Street 'cause they liked a
natter and would you believe it – they had the nerve to
open a theatre where you had to understand Yiddish –
what a gall! Many a time I'd been over there for a quiet
afternoon kip, paid my one and six and they'd say, 'You
understand Yiddish?' I'd say what you you mean 'Yiddish'
and they'd say piss off out of it!

LES: In the middle of London.

MIKE: It's not like a language . . . it's like a code.

DAD: You're right son . . . it's a bloody secret code.

SYLV: Do you know any dad?

DAD: Of course I do . . . I do know a bit . . . I went to night
school.

SYLV: Say something then.

DAD: Let's see . . . turn the cogs back a bit . . . uum . . . 'My
life!' That's Yiddish, that's four thousand years old that
phrase.

LES: Sounds English to me.

DAD: Of course it's not bloody English . . . it's four thousand
years old . . . that stems from the heart of Yiddisher land
. . . it's been fooling the bloody Arabs for years that phrase
. . . walking down Jerusalem high street they're all going,
'My life, my life'. They haven't a bloody clue . . . they
think it means something else . . . they think it means the
tanks are coming. Of course it doesn't!

LES: What's it mean?

DAD: What's it mean?

LES: Yeah.

DAD: I'll tell you what it means . . . My Life actually means . . . My Life!

LES: What's bloody secret about that?

DAD: I'm glad you asked that. You think that because it's a foreign language it's a foreign code . . . but it's not . . . that's the whole point . . . you get it! (*Pushes* LES *over*.) You dumb shmuck. Anyway, we'd go on the train on that hot Sunday morning, music playing in Liverpool Street Station (Still do that do they?) (*Sings 'We'll Meet Again' in falsetto*.) Vera Lynn. Magnificent woman.

LES: Yeah.

MIKE: She's dead ain't she?

SYLV: She's not dead.

DAD: Of course she's not dead . . . don't be so insulting! She's ninety-six years old, but she's not dead . . . she looks like she's dead . . . she sings like she's dead . . . but she's not dead . . . I went to school with her.

SYLV: You were at school with her?

DAD: I was at school in the same class . . . we were very close friends.

MUM: But you ain't ninety-six.

DAD: Of course I'm not ninety-six you stupid bonehead.

MUM: Well how could you be in the same class?

DAD: She was a slow learner . . . she didn't start her schooling till forty-three on account of disease . . . very backward . . . she used to sing all the time . . . what do you mean sending her up! She's done more for her country than you have. She's served in four bloody world wars she has. At the bloody front serving . . . what do you know about it you bloody raging suppurating faggot.

LES: (*Faggoty*) I don't know what you mean.

DAD: She was honoured by our great and glorious Queen. She went down to Buck House last week in our great and glorious Jubilee year . . . ninety-six years old . . . knelt before the Queen . . . she's not just bleeding old boring Vera from Bethnal Green any more . . .

MIKE: Oh, what's she now?

DAD: (*Authoritatively*) Sir Vera! (*Laughter*) You fell for that one
. . . well it's true. Anyway, Sunday morning Vera singing
in Liverpool Street Station, past Hackney and then head up
for the coast – what a larf we had then – candy floss, the
train out to the end of the pier singing 'Roll out the barrel,
we'll have a barrel of fun', listen to that!! Sung to the
rhythm of the train 'We'll have a barrel of fun' –
wholesome stuff know ya? – never knew what the pox was
in those days – didn't exist except on the blacks and no one
got near them or on a few scabby Chinese off the boats in
the West India Dock road. A pack of Woodbines was a
shilling and a pint was tenpence ha'penny.

MUM: (*From the distance*) Ninepence.

DAD: The oracle has spoken . . . what she say?

SYLV: Ninepence.

DAD: Ninepence! Ninepence! . . . She's right! She's right! I tell
a lie it was ninepence. Doris was all right in those days.
She weren't fallen apart with all that grease – makes you
sick. I wonder why women become such old cart horses
after they marry – after Mike came her tits dropped so low
they could be seen dangling at the end of her mini skirt
which she never should have worn – a mini at fifty! And all
she's got in her box is a space – you could climb in her for
a quiet snooze like the other night . . .

SCENE 14

Scene of the Two in Bed

MUM: Fred (*Pause.*)

DAD: WHAT? (*Pause.*)

MUM: Are you fucking me? (*Pause.*)

DAD: (*Dry*) No.

MUM: Yes you are – I can hear you!
(*Blackout.*)

SCENE 15

Mum's Lament.

MUM: He's a dirty bastard at his age. If he comes home pissed
out of his head he grabs me and calls me his doll – I'm
used to being left alone now – get no sensation no more –
years of neglect have taken away the edge – so when he
starts on me it's like being assaulted, it's dirty. We always
keep our underwear on – in bed – just his horribly belchy
breath – once he belched in my mouth as he was giving me
a reeky kiss – I slapped him so hard he let out an enormous
fart – that made me so cross I slapped him again and he
pissed the bed laughing – we haven't kissed since then. I
could still do it I've no doubt, just the desire's faded – I
almost did once – have an affair – a short one – I was in
the Poplar Cinema – just past the Troxy off Commercial
Road, it's now been condemned I think – watching Anna
Neagle in that beautiful film *Spring in Park Lane*. Some
geezer started to fiddle with my skirt and then touched my
suspenders. I was about to speak my mouthpiece when I
thought 'Shut up Doris behave like a bloke' – dirty like –
so I did. His hand was very slowly lifting my skirt up – so
slowly like he was afraid that at any second he'd feel an axe
come down on it – go on boy I thought, and he was only a
kid – fuck me, just a sweet kid of sixteen or seventeen –
couldn't see me in the dark and I didn't like to look – shy
like. So he took my hand rather boldly I thought – and
placed it on his chopper; cheeky! . . . and he had a
beautiful silky hot one, all ready primed and juicy – I was
getting ever so flushy and each time the usherette went past
we'd freeze like two statues – I kept on pumping away –
he'd be fumbling with my cami, my cami-knickers that is,
and then it shot out all over the back of the next seat,
whoosh!

(DAD *in the front seat reacts as if the great whoosh of sperm
had landed on his head – he says, 'Was sat!?' looks up as if
something has landed on him from the balcony and goes offstage*

mumbling things to himself like 'Something seems to be leaking out of my head.' MUM *then continues her speech.*)
The film had just ended – Anna Neagle was just making up with Michael Wilding, and he was wiping his spunk off the front seat, not Michael Wilding, this boy next to me. When the lights come on – Oh dear – I did turn queer when I saw our Mike – dirty bugger – takes after his dad – I copped him out when he got home.

SCENE 16

Les's Speech: A Night Out.
LES: I fancy going down the Lyceum tonight. I double fancy that.
(*The Lyceum music starts and* LES *and* MIKE *dance with invisible partners.* DAD *and* MUM *come on and dance in their own style –* SYLV *enters* MIKE *asks her to dance – the Andrews Sisters is played on a tape. The dancing of* MIKE *and* LES *is stylish '55 Lyceum style. A bar is created (*MUM *becomes barmaid.) Much drinking goes on. A fight nearly starts. Everyone leaves – then the two boys re-enter at a run, hit the centre spot, the music stops and the scene continues as before.*)
Being as it's Sunday we'll have Mr Ted Heath the famous band leader, not the acid bath murderer or notorious political impersonator cum weekend transvestite – and Dicky Valentine in a blue gaberdine, button two, flap pockets, hip-length whistle and flute. I'll wear a roll-away collar, a Johnny Ray collar, that sails out of your necks and a skinny tie – a slim Jim. French cuffs on the trouser with a fifteen-inch bottom. What about that handsome Donegal tweed with DB lapels? Button one, patch pockets, dropped loops, cross pockets on the trousers, satin lined, eighteen-inch slit up the arse on the jacket, skirted waist. What that one? Er– yeah – it's beautiful – finger tip length velvet collar, plenty of pad in the chest ('Come on Morry, I said, more padding'). Of course when we were geary we pulled –

not all slags neither, but you need wheels – no point in
pulling without wheels – or you'd end up taking some
scrubber down Edmonton and walking all the way back to
Commercial Road at three in the morning with as often as
not nothing to show for it except a J. Arthur reluctantly
given at the point of a seven-inch honed and sharpened shiv
menacing her jugular. When we got our wheels we pulled
handsomely a much better quality of cunt. There was not
much good quality cunt about then. And most of it were
from Billingsgate.

(LES *exits leaving* MIKE *in his spot.*)

SCENE 17

Mike's Cunt Speech.

MIKE: I disagree with Les. We always found good cunt at the
Lyceum. Friendly cunt, clean cunt, spare cunt, jeans and
knicker stuffed full of nice juicy hairy cunt, handfuls of
cunt, palmful grabbing the cunt by the stem, or the root –
infantile memories of cunt – backrow slides – slithery oily
cunt, the cunt that breathes – the cunt that's neatly
wrapped in cotton, in silk, in nylon, that announces, that
speaks or thrusts, that winks that's squeezed in a triangle of
furtive cloth backed by an arse that's creamy springy
billowy cushiony tight, knicker lined, knicker skinned,
circumscribed by flowers and cotton, by views, clinging
knicker, juice ridden knicker, hot knicker, wet knicker,
swelling vulva knicker, witty cunt, teeth smiling the eyes
biting cunt, cultured cunt, culture vulture cunt, finger
biting cunt, cunt that pours, cunt that spreads itself over
your soft lips, that attacks, cunt that imagines – cunt you
dream about, cunt you create as a Melba, a meringue with
smooth sides – remembered from school boys' smelly first
cunt, first foreign cunt, amazing cunt – cunt that's cruel.
Cunt that protects itself and makes you want it even more
cunt – cunt that smells of the air, of the earth, of bakeries,

of old apples, of figs, of sweat of hands of sour yeast of
fresh fish cunt. So – are we going Les? We might pick up a
bit of crumpet.

SCENE 18

At the end of the last speech the two boys return to the chairs –
MIKE *starts slowly to speak the song 'Daisy, Daisy Give Me Your
Answer Do' acting it out to* SYLV *who reacts favourably eventually.
They all join in until it becomes a fracas – at the peak of the noise
when all are jumping up and down and shouting –* MIKE *leaves the
group – followed by* LES *– they share the next speech – remaining in
the same two areas they opened the play with.*

SCENE 19

Resolution.
MIKE *and* LES. (*The lines can be split or spoken together, as suits
the actors.*)
    I'm sick of my house,
    I'm sick of my family –
    In fact they make me sick.
    I don't mind
    One day like the brothers Kray
    Like Reg,
    We'll be flying along happily –
    A chopper in one hand
    A dagger in my flute,
    We'll see the boys in Dean Street
    ('Allo son, I'll have a hundred suits').
    The East End's my manor,
    I mean that's what we know
    Trolling down the Green
    Bethnal to you –
    Going down the Lye –

The Lyceum Strand –
Kicking Cypriot berks to death
With Johnny and the gang –
Where's Big Harry gone? and Curly King?
Where's hard Arthur? Where's all the hard men?
Where have they been?
We'll open a porn shop,
A knocking shop too –
We'll spring the Krays, handsome –
The Richardsons too.
We'll threaten and murder,
Connive and rob,
The law's on our side –
We'll pay the slobs.
We'll get our piece –
We'll protect their bit of trade,
The hard porn and tit shows
They'll give us our pay
Every week.
We'll eat at Mario's where the
hairdressers go
We'll get fat, we'll kill and we'll knife
I hate all you pseudo bastards,
I hate you with my life.

SYLV's *Speech of Resolution.*

We will not end our days
In grey born blight – and stomp
Our hours away in fag end waste.
And kiss the minutes till they budge
While we toil in some stinking
factory – But what's the future lads
for us – where were the stars when we
were born that ordained that our birth
and death should be stamped out like
jelly babies in a jar to be sucked out
and chewed, then spat out at the end to

croak away before a flickering light
– and fill in forms at dole queues and
stand behind the sacks of skin that are called
men and women, translated into numbers
crushed in endless files – we will not end
our days like this – waiting, while ma and pa
make little noughts and crosses upon
coupons called hope-or-death – we will not
end our days like this.

MIKE: Bung us a snout. Les?

LES: OK Mike. I'll donate to thee a snout.

MIKE:
LES: } Now you know our names.

GLOSSARY OF SLANG

berk (Berkeley Hunt)	female pudenda
boat or boat race	face
bundle	fight
charver	sexual intercourse
china	friend
chopper	axe or penis
clobber	clothes
clock	pointedly look at
curly king	East End tearaway
double strong	keenly
flute	suit
give a kick	eye up
hickory dickory	time
J. Arthur (Rank)	wank
jellies	eyes
knuckle-sandwich	fist
Kray twins	East End murderers serving life
Lyceum	centre for hard tearaways in the late fifties. Formerly the theatre where Henry Irving played.
minces	eyes
mucker	friend
north and south	mouth
pegs	legs
pins	legs
pull	pick up
Richardsons	South London murderers serving life
snatch	female pudenda
snout	cigarette
sprach	speak
talent	good-looking bird
vardering	looking (early sixties gay vernacular)

WEST

or

WELCOME TO DALSTON JUNCTION

For Ian Albery, who made this possible

AUTHOR'S NOTE

West was first performed at the Donmar Warehouse, Covent Garden, in May 1983. That was its world première, although I believe a version was performed in Wagga Wagga, Australia, three years before, in 1980. But they had tampered with the text and even included a scene from *East*, thus disqualifying themselves from being the first to present *West*. *East*, my play about the East End from a young hero's point of view, was the first of a series which, naturally, inspired *West*. The BBC actually commissioned it and then found it not quite dull enough for television – much to my delight, as I was then able to stage it at a later date. Limehouse Productions and Ian Albery sponsored its first showing in London, and Limehouse have filmed it for television at the time of writing, so I hope that as *West* played before its thousands, it will soon play before its millions.

West is about courage: the courage to live according to your spirit and not the guidelines laid down for you by others, to be true to yourself, which may involve alienating others, but your truth is worth pursuing since it defines who you are. It shapes, forges and hones you into something that is not vague but clear-cut and definite. Mike's truth is to live for simple principles and to put his courage where his mouth is. He defeats the Hoxton monster and will continue to fight monsters so that others can rest safe in their beds. While the play is an allegory about demons we must defeat, it is also about an area of time and space called London and, specifically, Stamford Hill or Hackney, N16. You wore tailored suits and strutted your gear at the Lyceum, Strand, on Sunday nights. Movements were short, percussive and cool – Oscar Rabin led the band, Lita Rosa sang and the Kray twins would stand and survey their domain. I never saw them dance. Stamford Hill stood at the crossroads of Tottenham, Dalston and Hoxton and was subject to attacking forays from many directions. Such skirmishes were few, but I remember when, instead of sending a gang each time, Tottenham would send, symbolically, one of their toughest fighters to come and spread terror and challenge our leader. There was one young man from Stamford Hill who somehow elected himself to take on each one, and he did in fact beat them all. He was a frightening cur who actually put his fist through doors for practice. His name was Harry Lee. Mike is not based on a hero but is an amalgam of feelings that I had at the time and my observations of the environment.

West was first performed on 2 May 1983 at the Donmar Warehouse, London, presented by Omega Stage Ltd and Limehouse Productions Ltd. The cast was as follows:

RALPH	Ralph Brown
MIKE	Rory Edwards
KEN	Ken Sharrock
SYLV, Mike's bird	Susan Kyd
LES	Bruce Payne
SID, Mike's dad	John Joyce
PEARL, Mike's mum	Stella Tanner
STEVE	Steve Dixon
MESSENGER	Garry Freer

The HOXTON MOB are played by the same actors as Mike's gang with some subtle changes, i.e. cloth caps and chokers.

Director	Steven Berkoff
Designer	Nadine Baylis
Music	Mark Glentworth

A television production of *West* was broadcast by Channel 4 Television on 14 November 1984.

ACT ONE

Pub sequence. The stage is bare but for a line of chairs upstage whereby the cast act as a chorus for the events that are spoken, mimed and acted. A piano just offstage creates moods, adds tension and introduces themes. The piano starts up and the cast sing as the lights come up. They sing cockney songs out of order – 'My Old Man', 'I'm Forever Blowing Bubbles', 'Roll out the Barrel', 'You are my Sunshine'. LES joins in. Time is called. They exit from the pub, leaving the boys and SYLV. The GANG explodes on to the stage and freezes.

LES: Breathless, I was aghast when I saw / standing between the full moon and the blinking lamplight, this geezer / all armed, a certain aim he took / and felled the swarthy git from Hoxton with a deft and subtle chop / I never witnessed Mike I swear such venom and gross form in leather stacked / his coat stitched and embellished with fine lattice work of studs (to be more deadly when swung) no other weapon being handy like.

MIKE: Armed you say?

RALPH: From top to toe.

STEVE: From head to foot.

MIKE: Then you saw not his face?

KEN: He wore his titfer up.

MIKE: By Christ, would I had been there.

LES: He would have much amazed you.

MIKE: Very like, very like.

LES: His face / his rotten grizzly boat looked like a planet that'd been boiled in nuclear wars or struck by meteors / razed by hurricanes, criss-crossed by deep canals and rank defiles / those scars were mute but telling witnesses of battles fought with weapons / grim with deadly promise / and fought to bitter ends before the shout of 'Hold, hold enough!'

RALPH: No shout of 'Hold' was uttered then / not when he earned those lines / the tailor that did redistribute his face served his apprenticeship in Smithfield's bloody stalls / had habit of a thrust and chop to fell a bull and by the likes of this man's deadly cheeks / was put to death / no waiting time allowed / they fought until the streets were strewn in blood and bits of human flesh did gladden many hearts of sewer rats that night / or so I heard.

MIKE: He must be a right ugly bastard!

KEN: The face doth resemble the asshole of an elephant.

MIKE: A face like that won't launch a thousand ships or pull the scrubbers to their beds in Edmonton / Gants Hill / or Waltham Cross / so let him have his scars / his medals that he flaunts to all / to put the shits up any villain that doth take a fancy to him / for a bout of bundle round the back. That don't go down with me / you hear / you scum, impressionable as the tides that lick on any shore and gather up the muck and floating rubbers from some hectic night that others have / you who feed upon the blood that others shed / and wipe the bums of hard-faced villains / living by their very farts that you gulp down / and think you are so favoured to be near / that don't go down with me you chorus that exaggerate some slimy punk / as big in your esteem as you are small / when seen through normal eyes and not those / bent with envy / and weighted down with fear / would seem a normal sort of bloke / a fraction harder than the most at most / but not a raving Cyclops crossed with Hitler and Goliath thrown in as well / so pack up all this natter / and confess the utter wholesome gen [*truth*] you fancy not my chances with this Kong?

RON: Of course we doth, my dearest lovely Michael.
(*They walk on the spot.*)

LES: We were only uttering the like of what we saw / destruction of the King of Hoxton's hardy pack / you know that gruesome mob / they're hard men Mike / as tough as hobnail boots / from days and nights of doing bird and eating porridge within the flinty walls of Pentonville.

KEN: And Brixton.

STEVE: Scholars of notorious hatchet men of Broadmoor /
served their apprenticeships at double time in Parkhurst,
Isle of Wight, 'neath the twins / who taught them ultra-
subtle ways with carving knives.

RALPH: They're brought up hard / since snot-nose kids they
never knew / the softer life / electric blankets when you're
snug at night from pulling scrubbers / from the Locarno
Streatham / or the Ly / that cold walk back to home and
hearth / a glass of Tizer in the fridge and mum's left
chicken soup for you to nosh.

STEVE: A bagel warming in the stove.

RALPH: Those dulcet ways doth soften us Hackney lads.

KEN: Sure we'd be good for bang with gang upon a bird / or the
occasional toe to toe with hard-faced Arthur or blond tyke /
from Tottenham / I've seen you fell the best / but those
from Hoxton / they're not human Mike.

LES: They feel no pain / they don't wear coats in winter even.

KEN: Not to spoil their whistles / crush their shoulder pads /
they don't even like pulling talent / lest they disembark
their energy they wish to save / for making love to violence.

MIKE: So that's why all those tarts and slags come running to us
panting / drawers at half-mast when they see a lad from
Hackney or from Stamford Hill.

LES: (*Walking downstage*) Of course / of course / their blokes
just given them clobberings / and pints of crummy bitter /
if they're lucky / and a game of darts / a kicking if they get
in front of Arsenal *v.* Spurs on telly on a Saturday / their
day of rest from hauling bricks around the sites, to harden
gnarled hands to bunch into thick mitts or knuckle
sandwiches / to finish off a pleasant evening at the Royal,
Tottenham / they're not for you / I know you're hard
my royal Mike – the King of Stamford Hill / I've seen you
put your dukes through wooden shit-house doors for
practice.

RALPH: But those hands were made for better things / like
dealing royal flush and trump beneath the deck.

ALL: Right!

RALPH: Unhooking bras one-handed / whilst the other like a subtle snake seeks other pastures.

ALL: Right!

RALPH: Or making rude and gamey gestures from fast cars at thick-brained yobs from Romford / who in slow and worn-out bangers / can only yelp and scream vile insults lashed in hate / about the nature of our origin / and flash their rotten teeth / as we slide past in fast Cortinas.

KEN: Birds galore in black / squashed in and squeaking / flapping in their awesome glee at your horsepower man.

LES: So let's forget the bundle / let's scout out what muff walks lonesome streets tonight / and drag them back to forty watts of Eric Clapton or Queen.

MIKE: Swallow it, you mean! And wear a hideous yellow on my back / to strut before a wanton ambling nymph / that's what you see for me / Mike the King of N16 / I'll drown more villains than a mermaid could / deceive more slyly than old Shylock would / and set the murderous Hoxton King to school / can I do this and cannot get his crown / balls, where he Al Capone I'd pluck it down / now listen men of little faith / beneath my gaberdine and / poplin shirts / beneath my Crombie satin-lined with slanting pockets / there beats a heart of steel and will of iron / I'll crack open his skull / with this / I do a thousand press-ups every day and forearm curls / a score of chin-ups on the bar / have made my arms a vice to crush a bear / bench-press 300 pounds / those triceps aren't just ornaments you feel / 500 squats a day with poundage on my back of two grown men / have made my thighs the girth of oaks / and five score pull-ups on an inclined bench have carved a marble sculpture on my gut / feel / go on punch and break your fist on me you snively worms / just 'cause my mum fed me with bagels / cream cheese and rich bortsch you think I am a powder puff or soggy stuff thus to be shaped to humping ladies' underwear round retailers or flogging

94

stockings out of suitcases in Oxford Street or doing
knowledge on a moped with a dream of owning one fat
stinking taxi cab / and sit spine-warped with 30p upon the
clock / where to sir? To some ponce who vomits in the
back / or has a quick charver . . . no boy / that's not for
me.

LES: Our mind's made up.

STEVE: Yeah / let him come / we'll show them what we're made
of.

MIKE: That's the way. I see you now / straining like greyhounds
in the slips at Harringay / let's away / arm yourselves my
boys / the heat is on / those that do not fight with us this
day will think themselves accursed / they were not here /
get chains and mallets / choppers and fine steel / we'll give
those evil bastards something to feel / we'll wrap a warning
round their skulls / and they'll not bestride our streets no
more / their ugly mugs scaring the police horses / causing
our pregnant ladies to abort upon their sight and smell / no
more banter / let's go pell-mell to meet in heaven or hand
in hand in hell.

ALL: Smash! Splatter! Punch! Kick! Nut!
(MIKE *starts the words with a physical action appropriate to
each word. The others take it up until it becomes a
choreographic and vocal symbol of an advancing army. This
action reveals a casualty – one of the lads from Mike's gang,*
HARRY, *lies dying.*)

HARRY: Food for w–w–w . . .

MIKE: Worms, Harry . . . worms . . .

RALPH: Quick, have it away / afore the law doth mark us for
accessory!
(HARRY *dies. They race off, running on the spot, then
turn upstage and run to their chairs, leaving Mike's mum
and dad,* PEARL *and* SID, *with newspaper each side of
the table.*)

Mike's mum and dad, SID *and* PEARL, *in their room.*

SID: It says here – pass another cuppa Pearl / that last night

violent street gangs clashed / causing gevalt and misery / six
taken in with wounds / one fatal / caused by they say /
rough Gurkha knives and chains.

PEARL: It's not safe Sid to walk the streets at night / you'll want
some more toast with your eggs?

SID: No, that's fine.

PEARL: A piece more cheese?

SID: Those lousy gits are getting bolder every day it makes you
sick / the youth today / you got some Swiss?

PEARL: No, only Cheddar.

SID: That'll do / are all the fish cakes gone?

PEARL: You ate the last one yesterday.

SID: That's all you made!

PEARL: When I make more you leave them.

SID: So – they can't wait in the fridge and give a warm-up
underneath the grill.

PEARL: Tomorrow I'll make some more.

SID: Then it's too late / my yen for fish cakes may be gone.

PEARL: That's why you leave them if I make a lot.

SID: 'Cause you don't tell there's some remaining / I always
have to ask – you know I like them Pearl! A thousand
curses on their guts those swine / the youth today / they
don't know what to do but spraunce about.

PEARL: They're spoiled by overpay and telly.

SID: I should smile / filth that comes out streaming from the box
and films!

LES: (*As chorus*) Shit, cunt-face, scabby bollocks.

SID: Ugh! You couldn't take like years ago your family out / to
queue in one and nines and have a laugh / a sandwich in
the bag to munch between the films.

PEARL: You'd always have a laugh.

SID: That's right / you're right / feel safe and cosy / where's
little Mike?

PEARL: Bless him!

SID: He's tearing up and down the aisle / laugh! ice-cream from
Wall's at twopence.

PEARL: Choc ices.

SID: Ice lollies.

PEARL: Vanilla cup.

SID: Chocolate whirl.

PEARL: Bag of peanuts.

SID: Never ate them / stuck in my dentures.

PEARL: I did.

SID: Yeah, you did / all the way through *Road to Bali*, munch, munch.

PEARL: *Road to Singapore*.

SID: *Road to Mandalay*.

PEARL: *Song of the Desert*.

SID: *Wizard of Oz*.

PEARL: *The Red Shoes*.

SID: Beautiful, beautiful, what a picture.

PEARL: *King Kong*.

    (CHORUS *mime end of* King Kong *sequence* – MIKE *on table as Kong and* CHORUS *as planes shooting at him*.)

    Get off the table, Mike, you'll upset your father.

SID: That was a shocker / a cuddle in the back.

PEARL: You never!

SID: Didn't I? Yes I did – and then we'd have a cuppa in Joe Lyons with a pastry / right / they'd make a great cuppa then.

PEARL: They were famous for it then.

SID: The pastries were delicious then.

PEARL: They made the best then.

SID: Rum baba / chocolate éclair.

PEARL: Custard tart.

SID: Lemon meringue.

PEARL: A gossip with our friends all content like don't see them any more.

SID: They don't visit.

PEARL: You don't ring them.

SID: They don't ring me / I should ring them!

PEARL: They should ring us.

SID: That's right – never ask about the kids / never say like

years ago / come over Sid and have a cuppa, a game of solo
and a natter.

PEARL: You asked them once.

SID: I did / you're right / I won't keep begging them / I should
beg them! / What have they done for me? I ask myself.
Except to ask a favour.

PEARL: That's all.

SID: Hey Sid – lengthen a sleeve – Norman's grown out of
them / take in a seat / you couldn't put a new lining in /
could you?

PEARL: There's one in hospital who's still in coma fighting for
his life.

SID: They get what they deserve / what they sow / they reap /
they get as good as they give / I should worry for them? /
An overstretched health service / and they get a bed at
once / they should have let them bleed to death.

PEARL: He's still a son to some poor mother.

SID: Unwanted bastard of some brass no doubt / brought up by
waiting by the pub.

LES: (As chorus) When we goin' home, Dad?

SID: Outside the door in all weathers / waiting for his dad and
mum who's sinking down the pints inside / and now and
then peek out to see the kids all right / buying them a bag
of crisps to keep them happy / makes you sick / their little
noses running / blue knees and shivering / while ma
does . . .

(Chorus sings 'Knees Up Mother Brown'.)

. . . 'Knees Up Mother Brown' to some joanna that's the
life they had / witness the clouts their mums have suffered
at the hands of doltish drunken dad / and emulate the like
as they turn into them in turn / coming home from school
all starving with a bit of bread and dripping on the table
and a note / do not disturb / while mum performs with
'uncle' up the stairs / breaking in and entry in their teens /
and then a term or two of Borstal sets them up to be the
citizens of our fair capital / when once we walked down

Leicester's famous Square and had / the Corner House / a
quartet playing / lunch at half a crown.

PEARL: Those were the days.

SID: The Salad Bowl.

PEARL: Mixed Grill.

SID: The Guinea and Piggy.

PEARL: All you could eat for a guinea / imagine.

SID: I kept going back for more / remember? He couldn't
believe his eyes.

MIKE: (*As chorus*) You back again?

SID: Five times he saw me / fill it up I said / the plate was up to
here / I wolfed it down though / went back again / all you
could eat that's what it said / there's nothing they could do.

PEARL: They closed it down that's what they did.

SID: Not on account of me! 'Cause hard-faced layabouts would
lay about at night / and put the wind up decent folks.

CHORUS: Hey Jimmy, gie's a drink!

SID: That's why they closed it mate / the West End's now a
karzi.

(*Chorus mimes vomiting.*)

SID: Now you dare not walk the streets at night / lest some
unsavoury mugger / some huge shvartzer maybe / takes an
eye to you.

CHORUS: What you lookin' at?

SID: Or drug-crazed hippie dying for a fix decides to stick a
bayonet in your guts for half a dollar.

PEARL: I'm nervous going to bingo even and that's only down
the road.

SID: Nobody phoned, eh?

PEARL: No, shall I ring Rosie / ask them round for tea on
Sunday.

SID: We should ring them! When do they ring us?

PEARL: You're right Sid / you're quite right.

SID: Be independent / don't be proud to be a little independent.

PEARL: When you're right, you're right / maybe she rang and
we were out.

SID: So did she try again? / You'll make fish cakes tomorrow.

PEARL: Yeah, I'll make a load / only who will eat them?

SID: I'll eat them / don't worry / I'll eat them!

Hospital. A bed. The face of HARRY, *dying, quite still. The table is the bed.*

LES: It was our fault that little Harry fell / his memory shall be honoured for all time / stabbed in the field by coward's hand.

RALPH: This will not go unanswered / he shall be avenged.

KEN: Eye for an eye / tooth for tooth.

LES: We had them on the run / they fled beneath our might / but one fell rat draws out a knife to leave his mark behind.

KEN: The canker of the nether world / they are a plague that we must crush / or else they'll grow / contaminate by touch.

RALPH: What's the answer / blood for blood?
(*Music stops.*)

MIKE: You must strike at the top / cut off the head and then the body's dead / confusion then will spread about / then we mop up / to get into the hornets' nest and kill the king / not battle in the streets / but plan concerted armed attack / he's hard you say / invincible to some / but he's only a human like us all / with feeling senses / if you kick him does he not hurt / if you stab him will he not bleed?

LES: To go into the lions' den is begging for it / they'll smell us at a mile / they'll see our homespun spotless faces / not scabby / lined with tracks like Clapham Junction / they'll sus us out before we're even near and wipe us off the streets.

MIKE: A little camouflage is what we need / divest yourselves of your smooth gear / and imitate the clobber of that mob / cheese-cutters and football boots / a choker round our neck in white / a black shirt here and there / and dirty up.

RON: That's great / I'll drink to that / let's make a ding-dong at Dave's pad to celebrate this plan / you're all invited / bring some booze the birds laid on / some slags he pulled from Dalston double-hot in keenness / and mad to make acquaintance of you Mike.

KEN: Yeah I double fancy that / right on mate / I'll change my knickers / let's get the booze.

MIKE: Do not forget what we have said tonight / don't let this booze-up blunt our dreaded purpose.

LES: Nay! / We will speak further on it / oh come on Mike / let's mix our grief with some small joy / to celebrate destruction of the beast / we'll make our plans tonight and fix the day!

MIKE: OK, at the Duke's Oak we meet / that's on the way. (*Boys' pub talk*: 'Five pints, Bert.' 'Straight glasses, if you please.')

Mike's bird, SYLV, *in her room. Boys and family act as simultaneous background from their areas: pub at top;* PEARL *and* SID *in centre;* SYLV *at bottom.*

SYLV: It was November / the last dead leaves of autumn / were falling off the perch / the day was cold as ice / flawless sky mind you / like it was washed in Daz / the pigeons picking at the hardened chunks of dogshit / it's silent, like a Sunday is round here / and I went down the road to get the *Sunday Mirror* / and some fags / the OAPs were snivelling in their scarves they wrap around their sunken sucked-in cheeks / as they bought cat food for their sole companions / their chat was shrill with 'Hallo Dot and how's your chest' and 'Innit parky, half a gallon of paraffin' / and back they went swaddled in veins and rheumatism to their grim / stove on the landing / room / cold water and a pic of dad / when he was fighting for his king for three and six a week / a postcard on the mantelpiece from daughter seen just once a year / at Xmas maybe / or a death / it's funny that I sit in now and wait for him to ring / he said he would today.

MIKE: Go on, Les. Put something on the jukebox.

LES: What d'ya want – Rosemary Clooney?

PEARL: Must we watch telly all the time? Let's play cards.

SYLV: Mike usually decides to come over / that's so nice / we sit in watching some old flic on telly / or playing Perry Como or some Brahms particularly he likes the Fifth by

Beethoven / it gets him all worked up he says though / I
like dancing really to some Latin / we jump around a bit
and shake a leg / we'll have a fag or two / or smoke a joint /
maybe a benny just before our lunch / I'll warm a frozen
curry from the store / maybe Fray Bentos / though Chinese
from the takeaway is nice / some nice chop suey and some
chips / that's good, I fancy that and he don't half love it as
well / I'll get that in a minute and what else / I think that's
all . . . oh come on Mike and bloody phone you bloomin'
bore.

MIKE: Not too much, Ken.

KEN: Five more pints, Bert.

SID: Oh my ulcer! Pulverize a couple of pills, Pearl!

SYLV: Suppose I get it all and he don't come / I'll keep it for
tomorrow / I'll do that he ain't half nice – really he is / he
has his funny ways / I mean who don't / and sometimes I
could strangle him / but when he looks at me with those
hurt eyes / I just want then to mother him / he's really
handsome like a movie star / but rugged like not poofy but
a cross between Paul Newman and Brando / with little
hints of Redford and a touch of Cary Grant or maybe Boris
Karloff / he don't half make me laugh sometimes / we'd
laugh so much they'd knock back on our walls / those from
next door – that woman who is always sick and lives with
her mad son who never works / oh come on Mike.

MIKE: So go on, ask me: do I care?

BOYS: Do you care?

PEARL: Dorothy said she might pop in tonight.

SID: I'm out!

SYLV: I can't remember did I take the pill today or not / oh piss
I lost my little card / oh never mind / but then suppose he
wants to then what do I do / oh never mind one day won't
hurt or will it / no I shouldn't think it would / or would it /
rules are rules and if you break them then you take the risk
– men! Much they care – but then they're not supposed to
– really / they never do.

STEVE: Seein' Sylv tonight?

MIKE: Nah. Givin' her the elbow.

LES: How about Ange?

PEARL: Turn it off, for Christ's sake.

SID: It's the weather forecast.

SYLV: I can't go through all that again / no God forbid / I just
     can't go back to that vile place / and let them in to murder
     part of me again / like opening your doors to killers in
     white coats and saying / it's in there – you will be quick / it
     won't hurt it – will it? / No! No! Not again / oh come on
     Mike I'm getting bored hanging around – it's Sunday –
     come on ring you sod.

RALPH: So I said, pal, do I look like a tin of dog food?

SID: Go to bed.

     (SYLV *takes fag out – looks in mirror. Lifts her skirt –
     suspender belt, garters.*)

SYLV: Couldn't resist it really – he likes that – it's cheeky / I
     feel funny in the street / funny and nice at once / to know
     what's underneath / and no one else suspects / how could
     they / I'll give him a surprise / that's if he wants surprising
     that is / don't know lately if it's getting / well . . . / better
     or worse / can never tell with him / or maybe he's getting
     something else to play with / bastard bet he has / oh if he
     dares! Maybe that's it / it's wearing out / it's not the armed
     assault like once it was / then he'd come at me like I was
     the last bird in the world / he said he loved me then / after
     the op he turned all funny for a while / chop suey or a
     curry – maybe a plate of spags / oh ring you git I can't stay
     in all day and wait and wait.

LES: Here's to a smooth and slick funeral!

PEARL: It's just a blank screen, Sid!

SYLV: I fancy going up West / I'll treat him to a film and we'll
     sit in a nice wine bar / I'd like to meet some people / for a
     change / just watch them even / sick of staying in / oh come
     on, ring me, please ring! Please ring – please ring.

RALPH: Do you all know the way to Dave's? First right, first
     left.

PEARL: I'm going to bed.

The gang at a table – harsh white light.

MIKE: A score of broken bones and busted shnozzles was the price we paid by being unprepared.

RALPH: By being unprepared we was caught out with knickers well and truly down.

STEVE: They came back for revenge last night / for the almighty pasting that they took as if poor Harry's precious life was not enough to slake the creature's thirst.

LES: The brute and monstrous thing rose from its lair into the thick sulphurous night / while we were snoring gorged appetites like swinish pigs / well bloated and obscene from 'evening in' with favoured bints / their perfumed limbs enwrapped us like some marble seraphims / the sweetttnness of their breath, so honeydewed mellifluous with tinkling flute-like voices / beguiled us with soft porn suggestions / in the dales and valleys of our ears / and we unpeeled them like it was a ripened plum or mango – satsuma or sweet pear. But they were poisoned fruit / within they carried venom / between their loins a praying mantis / sucking us to our death in lust-filled swoons / for they had plans / the birds we pulled last night were fronted for attack / were set up to assuage us in our guard by rendering unarmed our finest men / attacking us where we are vulnerable / our sensual centres / famed to all the world / those cornucopias of passion / our Achilles' heel / our Samson's hair / where flock the sirens of the Western world / to feed and drink in our rich pastures / welcoming them all / turning none from our door / those starved within the barren regions / of Dalston, Enfield and Wood Green / who flocked to Stamford Hill.

MIKE: Oh horro! Horror! Horror!

RALPH: We planned too late our deed / we should have struck when he was bloated in his bed as he found us / instead of deeds / we fell to carousing as if to celebrate the victory before it's won.

MIKE: Oh you my sinews bear me stiffly up!

RALPH: We were a cinch / lucky for you that you were out / the

stroke of fate that did decide by tossing coins / you were
the chosen one to buy the shish kebab from takeaway / or
else you may have suffered that like fate / that marched so
painfully upon our undefended loins.

MIKE: My fate cries out and makes each petty artery in this
body as hardy as the hardest villain's nerve / I'll tear him
all to pieces!

ALL: You shall not go.

MIKE: Unhand me / by heaven I'll make a corpse of him that
lets me / I say away! I warned you / what did I say! You
were seduced by snatch / your watchman fast asleep / his
potion drugged no doubt / allowed yourselves to be
disarmed and floating in the ether of vile lust / so's not to
hear the hobnail boots they always wear with toes
steelcapped in dread / you mugs / what are you / with
friends like you I don't need enemies / you were
outshrewded by the Hoxton fiends / who's celebrating now,
no doubt in City Arms / carousing with his chinas of / how
easy it was after all / and laughing with loud chortles /
while the blast of shame sits on our brows like the ill mark
of Cain / now who comes here?

(A MESSENGER approaches.)

MESSENGER: I come unarmed from Hoxton's mighty King / to
give a message to him that calls himself / the Prince of
Darkness / the King of Stamford Hill or just plain Shtip-it-
in Mike.

MIKE: I'm known by many names but those will do / say what
your business is and blow / you emissary from the
underworld where sunshine never comes and days are
choked in hell's polluted smoke / say what brings you here
to gloat upon your master's cowardice and treachery.

MESSENGER: Cut out the patter man and cock an ear to what
my honoured master hath to spout.

KEN: You dare to speak like that you pint of gnat's piss.

MIKE: Let him go.

MESSENGER: And wisely said / that you may learn a thing or
three / I see you are the guvnor / so here's the spiel / to cut

all these wars which doth confuse the citizens of our strife-
warm manor / to halt the battles in the Royal Tottenham
which hath us banned from dancing with our chicks / and
making parley with our mates / to cease the clash of skull
and iron in our streets which doth excite old johnny law to
exercise his tool on us / and bring the black marias out like
wailing banshees / round our council flats / in other words a
one to one / just you and he – step round the back – by
some remote deserted track / the Hackney marshes / or
designate a place that you prefer / I'll pass the message on.

MIKE: The marshes suits me well / tell him I'll come.

MESSENGER: Upon the stroke of twelve / one week from now.

MIKE: I shall be there.

(MESSENGER *exits*.)

LES: I do not doubt some foul play.

MIKE: A one to one / it's what I've always dreamed of.

KEN: What if he should lure you into some forbidden trap and
there . . . phut!

MIKE: What should I fear / when I now sense a giant strolling in
my veins / now I could slay whole armies all alone / a one
to one / I wish there were a hundred just like he / a week
from now / till then sit still my soul / for Hackney marshes
will become the bloody sea.

(*They trot off in quasi-military fashion. Exeunt. Fanfare.*)

SID *and* PEARL *in their room. They speak but not to each other.*

SID: Soho's not what it's cut out to be.

PEARL: I get bored watching telly every night.

SID: There was a time when it was fun to walk the streets in
summer / birds out on the game / all legs / then to stand
about / flaunt themselves for all to see / you knew what you
were getting / not that I got / but for a laugh you'd ask how
much / and go up to the next / it passed the time.

PEARL: Sometimes I'd like to pack my bags and leave him to it /
just run out and go / I don't care where / just up and off /
and never see his face again / it's too late now / I should
have done it long ago.

SID: Where did it go wrong I ask myself / she never had to do a
stroke of work / I brought home all my wages every week /
not all mind you but they never went short.

PEARL: He's not taken me out in years / not once in years like /
come on Pearl let's drive to Brighton for the day . . .
(*Tableau as* BOYS *and* SYLV *join in and re-create the scene.*)
. . . it's sunny out / we'll pack a lunch and take the kids I
used to like it years ago / the pier and stroll along the
prom / sit on the beach and watch Michael throw pebbles
in the sea / and then a game of housey housey it's called
bingo now / we won a silver-plated teapot . . . (*Scene
disappears.*) . . . where has it gone I wonder?

SID: The others all made profits from the war / I was an honest
joe / I could have made a fortune / with a little simple
graft / black market was the rage.

PEARL: But for the kids / I'd have slipped out long ago / but
when you're tied it's difficult / how could I leave them / or
support them in a furnished room / it's just for them I live
– it's for the twinkle in my baby's eye that I can soldier
on / not that he's an angel but he's all I got / and she's as
good as gold.

SID: They're ingrates that's the truth / give us a quid or two
dad / or a tenner / or a pony maybe / pay you back? No
never / sponge on my old bones till I drop dead / I'd like
for once to see him looking smart / a decent hair cut / a
well-cut suit instead of that costume he wears / the
layabout.

PEARL: I look at him and think what have I got but habit and
some sleeping pills / to send us to oblivion at night or ease
the pain of our arthritic bones / to soften his loud snores
and give an hour or two of sweet forgetfulness / one day I'll
take the lot.

SID: Harry's boy did well / matriculated and all that / then
college / then degree in this and that / a clever lad / stopped
in most every night to fill his cop with knowledge / he's no
shmuck / and the skill to stand up in a court and be a
man / defending companies in the quagmire of business

laws / what a man is Harry's boy / his mum and dad he
bought a home in Chingford with a garden and drives a
Ford estate / what did my son achieve for us – gevalt and
anguish fear for every knocking on the door / in case some
johnny law should say we're looking for . . .

PEARL: Some wives have husbands who's a joy / so proud they
entertain / and lay a table for their friends on Sunday
night . . .
(*Party tableau*. 'Hello, lovely to see you', *etc.*)
. . . a drink of port / and tell some jokes / maybe a game of
pontoon / silver laid / and lumps of children everywhere /
daughters and sons / grandchildren too / to fuss over / their
grannies take them out / their fathers proud and braying
the achievements in the world of their most honoured
kids / they don't invite us any more . . .

LES: 'Bye, Aunty Pearl.

SYLV: Lovely meringues, Pearl.

MIKE: Ring you.

PEARL: . . . and I can't go alone / he says he's too tired to go
out / and what have they done for him he says / you've only
got to entertain them back / so we sit in and watch the
telly.

SID: I showed him how to earn an honest buck / I only told
him / get out now and graft / did I do something wrong / to
turn him to a villain / lousy sponger / low-life that he is /
who comes home when he does with busted teeth and
broken bones and God knows where he's been or what he's
done / if he stayed in and copped a book or two or got a
decent job when he was young instead of dancing out all
night with stinking whores no doubt / the filth he mixes
with is rife in bad contagion / if he had worked he's got
some brain / he could have been a manager at least of Cecil
Gee's / or maybe an accountant / Tucker that's a job! For
that you need a noodle in your bonce / faa! A pervert for a
son / to tell the truth no blood of mine but hers.

PEARL: He set him no example if he's bad.

SID: From her and all her spoiling he's no good.

PEARL: When did he get a father's love / I ask myself.

SID: She always favoured him / right from the moment he was born.

PEARL: He never took an interest in him the way a father should / to show him what it is that he should know.

SID: What time does *Hawaii Five-O* come on?

PEARL: Eight o'clock.

SID: Turn it on, will you love?

GROUP: I fancy going down the Royal / I double fancy that / the Mecca is my temple of fate / who shall I pull / who shall I meet, will she be wrapped up like a Xmas treat / the fireball is turning, the music starts / your eyes survey the crumpet / and you say, do you wanna dance, do you wanna dance?

BOYS: Do ya wanna dance?

(MIKE *takes* SYLV *on to the floor, just the two of them. The* BOYS *are upstage, acting as a chorus line with invisible partners.*)

MIKE: Do you wanna dance / we slid on to the floor like two seals in a pool / wearing an ashen look about her face / smelling like a perfume counter at Boots / she had that look about her / like I couldn't care if you dropped dead look / her eyes scanning other talent / searching out the form / of course we do not get too close / just enough to give a hint of things to come / a lasso of lust waves encircles her.

SYLV: He . . . he looks like any other / with easy grin / street-corner patter / so we dance a bit and then he asks me.

MIKE: Do you fancy a drink?

SYLV: With him / as if he bought me / for a dance / whereas I stand or sit with or without mates / watching lines of faceless trousers stomping up and down.

MIKE: She looks nice.

SYLV: He looks OK / nice eyes / love crumbled grey / and smoking already for me / he says he don't half fancy taking me home / back to my gaff / an arm squeezed.

MIKE: Fancy her / not much I don't half.

SYLV: Yeah another gin and it / lipstick smudged / I'll do my
hair / excuse me.

ALL: Thanks luv / that was nice / enjoyed that / fancy a drink /
where d'ya live? – oh!

MIKE: I got to the karzi / full of geezers doing their barnets and
who has who.

STEVE: I'll take the ugly one.

LES: Yeah all right!

KEN: What a cracker.

RALPH: I didn't get nothin'!

MIKE: And all that / I take the future of England in my hand
and ponder her body which seems to me as if a shoal of
silvery fish were gathered in a net / and wiggling and
slithery and her silken skin encasing her incredible form.

LES: Mind the strides, pal.

MIKE: Whilst I read what Kilroy has been up to / so after much
chat and I don't know / the night was wearing thin and I
became afeared that unless she yielded to my heart-felt
quest / to take her home that is / these chicks / these
panoplies of exquisite and sensual delights / would be
booked up by other snatch-bandits staking out their prey
for the night and if at twelve o'clock I walk home on my
tod sloan I would be well and truly choked.

SYLV: Not tonight, let it not be tonight.

MIKE: All right just to the door / unless . . .

SYLV: No, I said not tonight.

MIKE: Why wait / what makes it better if you wait / it's cold out
here / let's go inside / her make-up's cracked beneath the
light / our breath steams and snorts.

SYLV: He should wait / else I'm just another receptacle to stomp
out his butt / he pushes himself against me like I was for
him a sanctuary that he was struggling to get into.

MIKE: Like I was pursued by wolves / and she took my breath
away.

SYLV: And he asked me out next day / and from then on all I
wanted was to be a sacrifice / like an offering / I can't help
it / how often can you feel that / and that's how I felt / and

he felt good to me all the time / and often / not like the others but someone wanting someone like me / and now why won't the bastard ring?

The lads jump in attacking stance.

MIKE: Like stepping round the back was what was expected of you / like a clobbering now and then / was mixed up with pulling birds round there for stand-up charvers / like that very spot where now you gaily spray your spunk / was where two nights ago you splattered blood / 'gainst that very wall / you pulled in passageways / in doorways / in any nook and cranny so you'd only exercise your passion in the dark and private / with a bird / or bloke for violence or love / or be in love with violence / so when two tearaways decide to bundle / to inflict some GBH upon each other's form / they might be making love / and seeking out the soft parts to inflict upon them some unsightly woe / and finish off the night in blissful satisfaction / of adrenalin well pumped and flushy bleeding faces / all lit up with joy / and many hand thumps on the back.

STEVE: You did all right, mate.

LES: Yes? / you din half give him one / boot in like –

RALPH: Kicked the shit out of –

KEN: I liked the bit when –

STEVE: Well and truly.

LES: Handsome / ta da!

STEVE: See ya!

LES: Look after –

KEN: See you, plater.

RALPH: All the brest.

KEN: So he decided that it had to be and so prepared himself for the onslaught / toe to toe and nose to nose / the weapons chosen / and us chinas to be there in case the others thrust their grubby maulers in.

Gym. MIKE *training with weights / during this last speech / pushing weights in conjunction with music / muscles bulging / veins swelling /*

sweat pouring off in shower / the mates continuing their foreboding text.

RALPH: I've seen the brutish thing he has to slay fancy his chances / I don't know / I hate to tell my mucker / my best mate / that I might carry in my heart / a little doubt / so I'll keep shtoom / and render him my total confidence in this night's caper.

LES: The other bloke annihilated last week / was in a coma for some days / between the sheets he bled / and put tubes in both his ears / to see if he was leaking red from broken tissues / or the brain / that's what they do / and shoved up little things into his nose in case he haemorrhaged and formed a clot and shaved his head and searched his skull in case his mind was cracked / or broken / but he recovered to tell the tale.

STEVE: And was it worth it after all / I'd be rather all tucked up and wrapped around a softer creature / dragging kisses up from the deep / than face a bunch of fives well clenched / I do not fancy kissing that at all.

MIKE: But who can undo what has been done / or wipe the writing off from on the wall / what has to be will be.

Walking home after the gym, bag over shoulder. Music. Each one follows the other and takes over the walk.

RALPH: Walking home alone beneath the stars / up Amhurst Road / to Manor House / and down to Finsbury Park / where little ducks sit quietly at night / like toys in a lake of glass / to lonely back streets after / nights of rock and roll at the Rainbow / or James Bond giving her one at the Essoldo / Maybe a binge at some vomity local / going home in pairs / to make it in the back of steamed-up Minis / I could not help but wonder on this night of all the talent getting well and truly laid / and all the grinding going on / and how many and how much / and all the wails and screaming going on right at this moment / could almost in the silent aching streets / hear across the city all the sighs / rising and falling like sirens / thousands, maybe tens of

thousands creating a vast and lubricious symphony / a
concerto / and in the secret places / alleyways and back
rooms at parties / some in crispy beds / and some round
backs of lorries or in graveyards / some getting their oats
before their time / by dint of threat / in lonely fields /
dragged there by snatch-crazed fiends.

LES: Digging in and hacking away like crazy robbers / smash
and grab of flesh / and tides rising and falling together /
while the mad moon / a giant's eye spying it all out / the
murdered and the robbed / and geezers out for bondage in
Earls Court / and in the night the steam is rising / from the
heaps of bodies twisted in shapes like vampires feasting on
their prey / and the cars passing / occupants all warm and
cosy / he's driving / Zappa in stereo / hand on knee /
maybe one will stop for me / and some delicious and
horrendous piece / swathed in filth-packed flesh will utter /
can I give you a lift young man / drooling sibilantly from
scarlet lush-filled lips / opens the door / smelling like
honeysuckle in the dark the hint of things to come / the
promise of Elysium / and we'll shoot off into the night
searching for treasure.

KEN: But nothing / only the jeers of dawn carousers heading for
their unmade beds in Walthamstow and Leyton / reeking
stale beer and fish and chips / Fray Bentos pies from all-
night stands in Spitalfields / then home belching their
unholy gut rot into their scummy slags that hang around
hair lacquered like Brillo pads / and waking in the light of
day / one white arm / with digital / cheap one upon his
wrist comes snaking out the pit where scrubber lies a-
snoring.

STEVE: And searching in his trousers for a pack of fags / start
the day in cough-wake / dragging ropes of phlegm / from
vaults well stocked within / blue smoke rising / while the
sunshine peeks reluctantly in / exposing a big juicy yellow
pimple on her back / comes then spewing through the radio
some idiot / so the day starts in a bath of rancid bacon and
eggs.

MIKE: I'll get into my little bed / thus strengthened by steel for the battle ahead / I'll drink a pint / say my prayers / and wait for mum to wake me in the morning / French toast and tea / I double fancy that.

ACT TWO

Song of the Hoxton Mob. They march around the stage with East End macho-animalistic precision, jutting heads and threatening stares, to a drum beat.

CURLY:
> I'm known as the avenger / when
> they see me they do quell / for
> they see before their runny
> eyes a short pathway to ultra-
> violence / with a swift descent to hell.
>
> They scare before they get here /
> they tremble at my name / to look
> upon my face is quite enough to
> send them packing off before
> they've time to clench their
> sweaty fists to deal out pain.
>
> I'm known as the avenger / and they
> seek to claim my crown / but the
> hardest villains are the ones that
> soonest / come tumbling down.
>
> So come on boy / I'm waiting
> I hear you're on your way /
> I'm hungry for the blood of
> victims / I need another jerk
> like you / a mama's boy to slay.

MIKE *jumps into a pool of light and becomes a Cockney Lenny Bruce for five minutes.*

MIKE: Every day in the morning – while the sun rose like a
> biscuit behind the glue factory / quivering in the smoke /
> I'd get up at seven to go to work mum packs some

sandwiches / which would get soggy by the time it was
opened / I would crush myself in the tube and others
behind me would crush and we'd all get crushed together /
which was all right if you happened to have your leg
wedged between the thighs of some radiant fair-skinned
blushing and divine darling but not if some stinking
gentleman from an exotic country of the East was breathing
the shit he calls food all over your face / and as the doors
slid open this composite mass of sludgy flesh would wobble
like a wall of jelly / and some schemer would put a foot in
the door and attempt to weld himself into the compost heap
quivering together / on the Piccadilly Line poo! who
farted? was it you? I'd read the latest filth scrawled up
when the doors open no one would move to let anyone in /
we were staunch allies in our square foot of space / the
doors shut and the pack got squirmier / I was thinking
about that bundle all the while and making horrible little
flickers in my mind about the outcome / eyes staring into
their daily tits that they'll never feel only ogle / hands
would wander about in the pit of hell / old ladies gasping
their last breath / glaring at some young sod in a seat / and
umbrella stuck up your ass / fags stubbed out in your face /
and the ads advised you on the merits of speedwriting /
revealing some grotty slag smiling deliriously like an insane
gorilla / while chewing on an improvised cock drawn by a
future Picasso / and I stare all the time at the ads like it was
a meditation / while performing frottage against a piece of
taffeta / lovely / working as typist in Oxford Street / oh no,
don't get out yet / I'm not there yet / you may not be dear
but I am! / oh sod it / Oxford Circus / and the train heaves
us like a bad case of diarrhoea / then I'm channelled up the
elevator still holding my dangle / and briefcase with the
squashed-up sandwiches / churned up like the debris of
human rejects / bits of machinery on the conveyer belt
going back for repairing / or destroying / and I hoped I'd
see that bird again / she was lovely with great gooey eyes /
maybe I'll wait for her tomorrow / wend my way to my

office in Bond Street where I was a managing director of a
firm of wholesale jewellers / flogging pearls out of a suitcase
in Oxford Street for Xmas (genuine three-strung diamanté
pearls / a quid / with beautiful engine-turned, bevelled
edges / come on don't just stand there / gentleman over
there / lady over there / watch out there's a johnny / nip
into Woolie's or the ABC for a quick cup of bird vomit /
travelling salesmen swilling down some unidentified goo /
grins stitched to their unfortunate faces / collapsed spine /
frayed cuffs and souls / and breath to fell a dragon / I saw a
geezer shove his fork into a pie at one of these filling
stations / of garbage manufacturers / but it was empty
except for a mouse that was curled up inside with a happy
look on his face / sleeping / and he didn't want to disturb
the mouse like he thought it could have been a pet / since a
lot of these chain cafés have a lot of mice around / so he
took it back / this mouse has eaten my pie miss / she said /
this waitress who was slithering around in the dead grease /
with bunches of varicose like gnarled roots on her pins /
says: what and it's still alive! / I'm glad something likes our
pies / here never mind the humour I want another pie / he
was sweating now since he used this day's voucher up / she
says I'll send it back to the makers and if they find it faulty
they'll refund your money / but this didn't solve the
problem / and he screamed that they didn't need to send it
back / the evidence is there in the mouse / so after all the
rhubarb and shouting / he's kicking up a big pen and ink /
the manager comes sludging over / a fag hanging out of his
head / and one off his ear / and one up his ass no doubt / so
this greasy manager comes wiping his fingers on his apron /
since he'd been making ham sandwiches / had
distinguished himself in service by cutting the thinnest ham
in the world / and was straightaway employed by Forte's /
so here he was and said if you make a fuss like this in a
good British café / three million men fought the Second
World War on food like this / so the salesman bowing to
his superior size says all right / and the manager seeing that

the salesman had calmed down said / was there something
he could do for him / and the salesman brightened up a bit
says / perhaps you could warm the mouse up please /
certainly sir, right away sir, came the immediate response /
but the mouse sussing something is up with all the
movement going on cocks an ear and runs down the
waitress's leg / she screamed / farted loudly enough to
shake the windows and slides over on the greasy floor /
keeling over a table on the way down / whose aged
occupants were shocked into a sudden coma / well after
that I didn't fancy going back to that café any more / it's all
true / don't look at me like that / I'm worried about that
fight / anyway I gave up flogging bent gear in Oxford Street
after that / they say there's a big future in flogging
magistrates with bags over their heads / they pay well.
(*They all mime a tube in rush hour, the words of the* CHORUS
syncopating with the train:)

ALL: Breakfast, shit, work, lunch, bed.

*Back on the tube or walking the streets – slow motion – best on the
tube – only a few strap-hangers or passers-by become* MIKE'*s
friends.*

LES: Hallo Mike / I wish you luck for tomorrow.

MIKE: Thanks.

RALPH: How do you think you'll do?

MIKE: Very well thank you / how's your mother?

RALPH: She's OK.

MIKE: Still washing your knickers?

RALPH: No fear / I send them to be read by a fortune-teller.

LES: Are you scared?

MIKE: Not a jot / not a jot.

LES: I bet you are.

MIKE: How much / wanna see my pants?

SYLV: Don't go Mike / they're goading you on.

MIKE: What are you doing on the Piccadilly Line?

SYLV: Giving head to accountants in the rush hour.

MIKE: That's not very nice / is it?

SYLV: I waited in all day for you Sunday.

MIKE: I had things on my mind.

SYLV: That's what they all say.

MIKE: Who's they?

SYLV: I wish I knew.

STEVE: Going down the Royal tonight?

MIKE: I can't / gotta preserve my strength.

STEVE: Pity, we had something really dishy lined up for you.

MIKE: Keep it warm for me under the grill / I'll be back.

STEVE: You hope.

MIKE: What do you mean?

STEVE: Oh words words words.

MIKE: They're trying to undermine my fierce endeavour.

KEN: Hello Mike / coming for a ride up West?

MIKE: Not tonight Ken / not tonight old son.

KEN: Who's going with you Mike?

MIKE: I'll go alone unless you want to hold my coat.

KEN: Do me a favour / I wouldn't go down there for all the
salmon in Wentworth Street.

(*All except* MIKE *leave the train.* PEARL *and* SID *get on.*)

SID: You could have been an accountant or a manager of a
string of menswear shops.

MIKE: I'd rather be bounded in a nutshell and count myself
king of infinite space.

PEARL: Michael, my son, my joy and pride / jewel of my loins /
apple of my eye / the light of my life / the be-all and end-
all / the sun in the morning and the stars at night / where
are you going my son?

MIKE: For a fight to the death / a battle of honour / destruction
of a monster / to kill the plague / to slay the dragon / to
defend the weak / to prove my worth / to destroy the
mighty / to avenge the dead / to annihilate the oppressor /
to be a mensh / to have a punch-up.

PEARL: Well wrap up warm / it's bitter out.

SID: Come on, Mum.

(*They leave the train.*)

MIKE: Stars hide your fires / let night not see my dark and deep desires / maybe I'll go dancing after all to keep my mind off it.

The CHORUS *is seated as in a dance hall.* MIKE *takes* SYLV *into the centre of the floor. Gradually the others dance around them, holding invisible partners.*

MIKE: Do you wanna dance / I took her on the floor / the crystal ball smashed the light into a million pieces / a shattered lake at sunrise / the music welled up / and the lead guitarist / plugged into ten thousand watts zonging in our ears / callused thumb whipping chords / down the floor we skate / I push her thigh with mine / and backwards she goes to the gentle signal / no horse moved better / and I move my left leg which for a second leaves me hanging on her thigh / then she moves hers / swish / then she's hanging on mine / like I am striding through the sea / our thighs clashing and slicing past each other like huge cathedral bells / whispering past flesh-encased nylon / feeling / all the time knees / pelvis / stomach / hands / fingertips / grip smell / moving interlocking fingers / ice floes melting / skin silk weft and warp / blood-red lips gleaming / pouting / stretching over her hard sharp and wicked-looking Hampsteads / words dripping out her red mouth gush like honey / I lap it up / odours rising from the planet of the flesh / gardens after light showers / hawthorn and wild mimosa / Woolie's best / crushed fag ends / lipstick / powder / gin and tonic / all swarming together on one heavenly nerve-numbing swill / meanwhile huge mountains of aching fleshy worlds are drifting past each other holding their moons / colliding and drifting apart again / the light stings / the journey is over / the guitarist splattered in acne as the rude knife of light stabs him crushes his final shattering chord / the ball of fire stops / and I say thank you very much.

SYLV: OK.

MIKE: Speak again, bright angel.

SYLV: I fink I'll have a gin and tonic.

LES: You're avoiding your destiny by diversions.

MIKE: Tomorrow and tomorrow . . .

SYLV: I waited for you all day Sunday.

MIKE: I had something on my mind.

SYLV: Come on home / I'll cook you a plate of spags.

MIKE: I'd rather eat the air promise-crammed.

SYLV: You must be starving.

MIKE: I'm preparing myself for the battle on Sat.

SYLV: Will you come over after?

MIKE: Yes long after / if I am here.

SYLV: Are you scared?

MIKE: Not a jot.

SYLV: Why are you so mean / you told me you loved me once.

MIKE: You were the more deceived.

SYLV: Heaven help him.

LES: Oh blessed Mike / why art thou not in constant training for the event?

MIKE: How do you know what I do all day / who watches my mental exercises / detects the secret plans I make / an armoury of weapons / stored in the forceful regions of my brain / I'll hypnotize the beast / and psych him out / drinks all round.

LES: Here's to the end of the Hoxton King.

RALPH: Destruction of the stinking dragon.

STEVE: The ogre falls.

KEN: Hideous and most sweet revenge.

LES: No more trembling in the strasser.

RALPH: Pull the birds we like.

STEVE: Safe conduct to the supermarkets.

KEN: Unimpeded entry to the Essoldo.

LES: Sleep tight at nights.

RALPH: Noisy mouthpieces / no frighteners.

STEVE: No knifing from bumper cars at Battersea.

KEN: Our motorbikes safe from slashing tyres.

LES: No more dreaded smells.

RALPH: No more terrified cats.

STEVE: Shaking OAPs.

MIKE: The Hackney marshes.

ALL: The Hackney marshes.

PEARL: You could have been had you tried / a manager / a solicitor / or even a representative of a firm of ladies underwear manufacturers / your uncle would help you / I'm sure you would have liked getting into ladies underwear / look at your cousin Willy.

STEVE: Wife – three kids – responsibilities.

KEN: House in Colindale.

SID: Detached.

LES: Mark 2 Cortina – £15,000 a year.

(*They follow* MIKE *as he runs away from the train of responsibility that pursues him, and they circle stage and sit.* MIKE *whips round and makes a speech to the audience.*)

MIKE: Why should I yoke myself to nine to five / stand shoulder to shoulder with the dreary gang who sway together in the tube / or get acquainted with parking meters / be a good citizen of this vile state / so I can buy an ultra-smart hi-fi and squander fortunes on pop singles / what do you do at night between the sheets but dream of mortgages and oh dear the telly's on the blink / we're going to Majorca again this year / you who've never raped a virgin day / with adrenalin assault upon your senses / but aggravate your spine to warp / while grovelling for a buck / or two / smiling at your boss / and spend heart-wrenched hours at the boutique deciding what to wear / ragged up like Chelsea pooftahs / or chase some poor mutt on Sundays / mad keen to commit some GBH upon it / and birds like screaming hyenas with teeth and scarves flying / make your usual boring death-filled chat in smelly country pubs / with assholes like yourself / no that's not for me / I'd rather be toad and live in the corner of a dungeon for other's uses.

The HOXTON GANG *with their leader,* CURLY. *They appear to lean against a lamp post, each facing out, like four gargoyles, a hard light from overhead.*

CURLY: Night and silence / that's what it's all about.

BURT: You're right Curly / oh son of night – the atmosphere is double-strong / star-filled / the perfect evening for a fight.

PAT: It's what you need / a cobbled street / just wet a bit / to give a little image of a broken moon / a yellow lamplight / flickering a bit / still lit in gas.

REG: The echo of our studs on lonely streets / the smoke of cigarettes / thickening in a blast of light / like fiery dragons / in our lair we hover / smelling blood / our leathern wings glistening in the dewy air.

CURLY: The odd moth hanging about / and eyeing up the scene / banging his fretful wings / oh let me in it says / to the hungry flame.

BURT: Then out he goes / like a light double-choked / to be so scorched up.

PAT: Right burnt up he was about it.

ALL: Laughter – cackle – silence.

CURLY: In just such a manner doth our fretful moth of Stamford Hill / bang against the light that we give out / he wants to be let in / and then . . .

PAT: Phhht!

CURLY: We wait / we've time / I don't think he will be late / I sense him now weighing up the scales of chance / thinking thick regrets / and oh what a mug am I, swallow it, he thinks, turn yellow / at least you'll keep your face / the one the birds do like to chase / you'll lose the other / the one you'll never again show to mates.

PAT: He's as chicken as a chicken coming to a fox / his pants hot lined in shit / I hear / that fear has wrenched from out his guts.

BURT: He does it to be king of his bankrupt domain / to cancel out the bum he is at home / so he can spout out to the world that he's got clout / and make the teenyboppers moist their flowers / and holler, oh Michael / so he can stand up West and join the firm of grievous / rape / robbery and death / solicitors to the realm.

PAT: He desperately wants his diploma / and that is you / to launch him on the path of hate / that's lined in gelt and not a caper down the Ly / a bundle for a laugh / but turn pro / that's his game.

CURLY: I'll not disappoint him / I am guaranteed against default / reckless in my desire to give value / fear no marks upon my well-worn face / have nought to save / but welcome all / I'll make love to him / my caresses will start their long journey in hell / he'll not see it coming / only feel / I'll embrace him like a hungry bear / my hands will find his body's treats / and practise on his bones / we'll dance and then I'll look into his eyes / wet with tears of thankfulness / as I do renovate the house he lives in / he'll whisper like a gasping lover / to the background of splintering sounds / as he hears the music of his body's walls snap and crack / his heart will beat a terrible drum / and want to burst to spread some numbing death relieving darkness / so come on scum.

The café of Mike's mates.

LES: Two teas, Joe.

JOE: Sugar?

LES: One, ta.

RALPH: Got any sandwiches?

JOE: Sold out.

RALPH: Do you suppose it's possible to organize one?

JOE: Not now.

RALPH: Why not?

JOE: Because it's late.

RALPH: Ah, go on, don't be a fat pig.

JOE: Closing.

LES: Sod you, you slimy middle-aged fart.

RALPH: I hope you starve / the time will come when nobody comes in this dung heap and your family is condemned to catch rats to eat / while your children crawl in lice and your wife's hair falls out / may your daughters be gang-raped by blacks / and your house burnt down with your kids screaming / while you sit here counting your gelt you scheming piece of dogshit.

(*Record on juke-box: 'You are the sunshine of my life'.*)

JOE: All right I'll make you a sandwich / what do you want?

RALPH: Roast beef and coleslaw in toasted brown.

JOE: Just watch it / next time you'll go too far and say
something you'll regret, OK?

STEVE: Half-hour to go / Mike cut his hair and greased it / he
can't grip that / so as to introduce his knee upon Mike's
head.

KEN: That's shrewd.

STEVE: We should have been there / we should.

RALPH: Then why weren't we / case the others jump him if he's
out in front?

STEVE: Dunno.

RALPH: You're his mate aren't you?

STEVE: Well, so are you.

RALPH: Yeah.

STEVE: He's mad to go / what does it prove / to swallow it's no
shame / we know Mike's tough / ignore those bums / that's
what I say.

KEN: He'll swallow nothing / so he'll taste nothing bitter in his
mouth like us / he goes because he has to / and for us / you
know that's true / he goes for you!

SID *comes downstage, alone.*

SID: Once in Soho, a while ago, round the back streets / walking
one night to catch the tube I wandered round the
alleyways / a saunter for no reason but to stretch my pins /
up in the window was this bird / a right cracker she was / I
stopped and caught her staring down / a red lampshade
that tells all I don't know why / but I was tempted by all
the mysteries that glow foretold / I pretended to be staring
in the shop below / transistors and electrical equipment /
but up above was the socket I needed for my plug / a card
said 'Sally, two flights up' / I found myself upon the stairs /
grim smells and rot / knocked on the door.

SYLV *at home pouring a drink, upstage.*

SYLV: I hate to drink alone / sometimes I must / it quells the energy I have which I'd rather spend on someone / some him / or him / he leaves me with it bottled up and spare / I drown it out / my youth is going up the spout / in love that's wasted / I hate to stay in alone / how many others are like me / alone in boxes / waiting for someone or the phone to ring / what's the use to wait / and if he does / a thing of shreds and patches.

SID and PEARL *downstage*.

SID: So well, I knocked upon the door / and this scrubber opened it / looking like nothing on earth / while far below it was a mystery / I thought / she smiled / and showed a gap or three / the rest was black / and on her face a cake of slap / one inch thick at least / I thought I can't do this / I had my wages in my belt / not much since times were hard / and mum needed the gelt / for rent and clobber for the kids / a coat as well / but even so I couldn't now turn back / I hurtled through a quick time for . . . don't ask / it cost a bomb.

PEARL: You promised, Sid, you said I could have a new coat.

SID: And found myself outside the electrical store / and nothing to show except a rancid shag / and wages short / felt sick and empty / I couldn't buy my wife her winter coat / I sacrificed my wife for that / I'm sorry Pearl, I said, I earned a few bob less / you'll have to wait a week or two / felt real vile / she said.

PEARL: You promised Sid / you said that I would have a new coat Sid, this winter / that's what you said.

SID: I know / don't go on / don't start nagging / I sweat out my guts for you / I break my balls that you should not go short.

PEARL: Don't shout in front of the kids!

SID: I sit down by a bench all day / machining trousers for five bob / and dust choking my lungs / and the noise of the machines / you wouldn't believe it / and fifty in a room / ten pair of pants a day / I slog to make / cut and trim / then throw them to Greek to finish off / and put a fly in / and at

the end a Mick to press them / I got callused hands already
from the shears / a spine that's curved forever / and a
cough that can't be cured by all the medicines in the
world / that's known to man / to make a haven for my
family / which is a little heaven / so don't get on my tits.

PEARL: OK / I'll wait / sure I can wait / wanna cuppa?

SID: I wouldn't say no to nice cuppa, Pearl.

PEARL: I hope Mike's OK / I haven't seen him since yesterday.

SID: Does that surprise you / you look surprised as if that's
new / that he appears when you see him and not before / a
plague he's been to me (*To himself*) . . . it cost a bomb.

PEARL: What did?

SID: Nothing, what did I say?

PEARL: You said it cost a bomb.

SID: Oh I was miles away.

In the café, or MIKE *walking. The following can be said either by a
chorus of* LADS *or by* MIKE, *lecturing the* LADS' *still faces. For
continuity,* MIKE *should be alone.*

LES: At least the joy of being strong.

STEVE: Of owning your own body.

RALPH: Your capitals, your guts.

KEN: In your hands you hold the pleasure or the pain of the
Western world.

LES: Hands can be the instrument of life.

STEVE: Or death.

RALPH: What's it to be?

KEN: Either way you have to choose.

LES: You who watch and never had a choice.

STEVE: You look the only way.

RALPH: How many times did you want to lash out?

KEN: Give vent to what you felt?

LES: The bile that's choked within.

STEVE: Instead ate humble pie.

RALPH: How often did you want to impress the missus?

KEN: Be Charles Atlas and kill the dragon like St George?

LES: And how often did you tremble in your socks?

STEVE: Afraid in case you lost . . .

RALPH: Or broke a nose.

KEN: Ooh, painful.

LES: Damaged an eye even.

STEVE: There's lots to fear.

RALPH: And swallowed some offence.

KEN: A mouthful of slagging vile.

LES: And wished next day . . .

STEVE: When safe at home that you had taken chances.

RALPH: A memory to chat about on wintry nights to all the
kids . . .

KEN: Of how you were a hero.

LES: For a while.

STEVE: Never mind, you made a bomb in wholesale and made a
fortune in the market like a lucky Joe.

RALPH: Beneath it all you wanted at some time to be a hero
with your dukes.

KEN: To emulate John Wayne.

LES: Or other prince of celluloid.

STEVE: Because that's your courage that you stake.

RALPH: Your guts you gamble on the street.

KEN: Opposing some hard tearaway.

LES: And whip him.

STEVE: That's worth a lot.

RALPH: You know it in your heart.

KEN: How many carry an emblem of some shame . . .

LES: Some insult not yet purged away . . .

STEVE: That gnaws your very vitals?

RALPH: You forget, you say! Ignore that cad.

KEN: Don't get mixed up with riff-raff, darling, says your dolly
bird.

LES: You jump into a cab.

STEVE: Agree with her . . . they're not worth it.

RALPH: Ignore the mob.

KEN: Yet underneath it all you wish there were a Bruce Lee
tucked away.

LES: Or a Mike.

STEVE: Instead you pour a drink and gas about an incident at
    school when for a minute you stood up to wrath.

RALPH: You play the incident again.

KEN: And yet again.

LES: Re-run the entire scene.

STEVE: Imagine what you would have done . . .

RALPH: Had you the chance again.

KEN: Let him say it once more, you utter in your dreams.

LES: Too late.

STEVE: And if you had the chance again . . .

RALPH: Wouldn't it have been the same?

KEN: But knights are born not made.

LES: The others stand round and watch.
    (*They march off as tight group and comfort* MIKE.)

MIKE: See ya tonight then.

RALPH: Bird's in the club.

STEVE: Don't feel well, Mike.

LES: Gotta fix me scooter.

KEN: Me mother's sick.

MIKE: Don't let me down, will ya?

ALL: Course, Mike, yeah, etc.

Sylv's pad.

SYLV: What are you doing here?

MIKE: Aren't you pleased to see me / I had to see you / wish me
    luck / I got a little flicker in my guts / I must confess.

SYLV: Of what?

MIKE: Doubt and sick all mixed.

SYLV: Then don't go.

MIKE: Have to.

SYLV: Why?

MIKE: Sylv, the Fates have wrapped me up / to be delivered this
    night / I've got to go / revenge is one / strong one for a pal /
    as for the rest / what else is there to do / sure there is
    always a day that has to come / that you would much rather
    avoid / postpone / and send a card / forgive me / but / I
    can't make it this week / you lie in bed and sweat / hope

the daylight never comes / it's not tomorrow any more / it's
now / the readiness is all / but after if I'm still around / I'll
pop on over.

SYLV: I wanted much more than that / the occasional hallo love
and how are you / you busy tonight shall I come round / to
sit and wait is not my idea of paradise / in case you decide
this is the night that you decide to come / and what do we
do but pass the time until it's time to go and 'see ya! Be in
touch!' / I'd like to be there for a man / who lives for the
moment / so I can live for the moment too / when we can
meet / and protect that which we grow together within me /
not here love – here's a ton / go get it fixed / a hundred
quid to kick it out / buy back the space I'd rather fill / a
hundred quid / to kill / that's easy for the man in love with
death and pride / you are more keen to see your Hoxton pal
so you can be a tearaway / the King of Stamford Hill / if
you gave me as much as you give him / I'd be so happy / if
I obsessed you half as much / you'll give each other all the
thrills you are afraid to spill on me / you are in love with
him not me / so go enjoy yourself / be free / far easier for a
hand to make a fist than hold it open for a caress / easier
for you to smash yourself into his body than to mine / to
make yourself into a ball of hate wound up / so you can
hide yourself from what you fear / be a hard man / 'cause
hard covers the soft / the soft that's underneath is what you
fear / my woman's body tells me / is soft to make things
grow / its softness breaks down your rocks / can destroy
you like water wears down stone / go to your lover Mike /
go, and don't come back / go / be alone / and who will put
you together again when you're a pile of broken bones?

MIKE: Thank you very much / I'll bear in mind all what you
said / I spit out all my angst / confess my guts / wished I
had bit my tongue first / before I let those soppy words
crawl out my gob / I had a shred or two of doubt I do
confess / and that is all no need to make a song and dance /
accuse me of some vileness in my act with you / it takes
two to tango / don't forget that / anyway I'm here aren't I /

I come to you don't I / there's no one else / at least . . . you
get the best / sometimes the worst / that's what it's all
about / that's how it goes / that's what they spout in church
even / for better or for . . . / I'm sorry you don't find me
your ideal / you never will / you birds have scored into your
head / some geezer all identikit / a mister right / but they
never can and never will fit the little pictures that you
make / so without more ado / I'll take my leave of you.

Street.

MIKE: Didn't wish me luck even! I dunno / I'm all alone, that's
how it goes / my mates have fled / left me for dead / and
most pernicious woman left me too / I need a friend / need
somone / something / just to tell it to / tell me I'm OK /
I'm good / nah I don't need / anyone / I need revenge /
that's something to get on with / that's a start / don't take
away my *raison* dirt track / don't take away my art / I'll be
myself again / but now a numbing sickness is sliding down
my gut / I'll force it back / I clench my fist / it feels like
jelly / like a baby's paw / if only I had the strength of a
kitten I could win / I see myself reflected in a
windowpane / a death's skull stares me in the face / where
is my resolution / where the spleen that had me think I was
the king of the master race / bearded with the sweat of
fear / a demon came and sucked my blood / they sense
victims and hover like bats / the filthy beasts / that's all
right / who ever felt happy before a fight / you go in sick
but once you start and get the first sting in / your face you
then forget your problems / like an actor on the stage /
scared shitless in the wings but once he's on then he's the
king.

(CHORUS *rushes on – reflects* MIKE's *walk upstage.*)

OTHERS: (*At random*) You can do it, Mike.

Didn't wish me luck even.

How do you think you'll do?

He's mad to go.

No blood of mine.

But hers . . .
One minute, Mike.

LES: Hackney marshes.

(*The* CHORUS *leaves the stage.* MIKE *is alone. He acts the battle.*)

MIKE: He hits me with a hook / I'm down / a bolt to fell an ox / crumbles slow / then smashes me with a right / and now / I sway / a drunk looking for a hold / a volley a hard straight comes whipping out / smashing home / I go down slow like the *Titanic* / but grab hold on the way / and drag him down leaking red from all openings but still I hold him / close / he can't be hit / too close / and with my almighty arm I lock his neck into a vice / where do I get the strength / the brute's amazed thinking it was all done / but finds his head being smashed into the wall / but like he's made of rock / he twists himself from out my grip like some mad demented bull and snorts screams and kicks but by this time I dodge the sledge hammers and hold him at bay / alive again as if the blows have woken me from some deep sleep / I'm myself again / we move and circle / it's quiet as the grave / all tense waiting / the beast kicks out and hard / I grab a leg / and down he falls / hard / but with almighty strength the brute is up again / sneers and foams / and rams his fingers round my throat / grips hard / the others round about / screaming / kill the bastard / tear out his guts / and rip his balls off / I pull off his wrist and then we twist / fall / rolling / each trying to find a hold / and lashing out from time to time / knee / elbow / head / boot / whatever finds itself unoccupied and free for service / we break away and stand streaming like two dragons breathing flame / fighting to the death / each waiting for the other to move / still / just the sound of breath / then in the beast goes and fast and throws himself on me like to annihilate me once and for all / I go flying back thrown by the mass of hate and crash both down in a welter of struggling seething flesh / twisting foaming heaving screaming / I'm stomped on / sounds unearthly are heard / I fear it must end / and bad / he's on my chest / his fist drawn back / one horrible almighty gnarl of bone and brought it crashing down on to my face / pow and then again pow and now again pow / I can hear the sickening crunch / but I protect what how I can / draw energy from the deep and thrust my hand up underneath his jaw / with the other I smash it home / the brute stumbles / pulled off balance / my face is crimson blind by blood / I wipe with one hand / I'm upon him now spraying his blood on both like we were swimming in it / this time grip his throat and hold it fast / tight / tighter / after long time we topple over / again / rise slow like prehistoric monsters / the beast screaming / words / spitting out / no meaning / splattered curses / he bows like to pounce again / I then kick / it lands home dead square in the face / then follow up both hands working like pumps / like you never saw.

CHORUS: Pow-pow-pow-pow-pow / pow-pow-pow-pow-pow!

MIKE: But you wouldn't believe the strength of the brute / inhuman like / grinning like a gargoyle / he stands there, says come on do something / and charges again / I can't believe / as if my own powers mean nothing / see hopelessness and fear now flooding in as fast as strength is flowing out / we grip each other for a hold / to throw one or the other down / but I'm losing all belief / I'm down / as if it's better there / just lie covering my face / I'm kicked pow / once twice pow / feebly attempt to rise pow / kicked down / the fourth time in his glee / too keen, he misses / slides over on the blood slippery deck / heavy as lead / I climb up in agony / but do not miss the chance / to connect the monster's head with a bone-shattering well-aimed knee / it stops him dead / it looks surprised / astonished / and for luck / throw all my weight into a right which crashes open all in his skull / out go the lights pow / the Hoxton King keeled over / toppled / crashed down / in one terrible long rasping blood gurgled moan / then it was over / he twitched / raised his head / spewed between his bloody teeth the words / 'Nice one' / then lay quite still /

the lads about looked sick and pale / were shattered in their
souls / and thought the future black / I wiped the blood
away / put on my coat / they parted quickly from me when I
left / I staggered into casualty at London Hospital who fixed
me up.

*Gang as group like cheerleaders. They trot around the stage to give
him a hero's welcome.*

MATES: Well done and welcome home / you done us proud /
  terrific / so we heard.

KEN: Report was trumps.

RALPH: From far and wide.

LES: Your triumphs sung to the four corners of the manor.

STEVE: You look a mess.

ALL: But hold your head up / you're the ace.

MIKE: Oh yeah / my nose is broke / my lovely profile's gone.

RALPH: You'll get it back.

STEVE: You'll look better than ever once it heals.

KEN: Don't you fear.

LES: Sensational it were, I swear.

RALPH: My heart was out there for you . . .

STEVE: Stomping in my chest . . .

KEN: Like fifty insane drummers.

LES: When you got up and curled your right . . .

RALPH: I said a little prayer for its journey into space.

ALL: He didn't know what year it was / he didn't care!

MIKE: So where were you, deserted me ye men of little faith /
  all mouth and trousers when it comes down to the crunch /
  you could have shown a face at least to plonk your minces
  on the scene should tricky business raise its ugly face /
  instead you wait for news of my impending fate / it's over
  now / it's done / so what's it all about / I've had enough of
  this / I'm out.

MIKE *creeps into his house – enters Pearl's and Sid's room for the
first time.*

MIKE: Hallo.

SID: What the . . . ? Look at your face.

PEARL: Mike, oh God, what happened to you?

MIKE: I had a fight . . . but I won . . . I did it.

SID: So, look at you, what do you want / a medal?

MIKE: No / I just wanted to tell you / it's the last one I'll have.

SID: So tell me something new.

PEARL: Leave him, Sid.

SID: He's proud / he comes in here to tell us he's proud.

MIKE: It was hard / yeah I'm proud / his gang did up little
    Harry.

SID: Don't give us this talk / this time of night / your gang
    warfare / a ganster I've got and he comes in yet like he's a
    hero.

MIKE: I just wanted to talk to you.

SID: So / you've talked.

MIKE: I needed to tell someone.

SID: So you've told me / what do you want us to do?

MIKE: Nothing, just nothing you miserable lump of complaint /
    that's all you've done all your life / what else are you good
    for / nothing / and you give nothing / I've listened to your
    miserable snivelling complaints for years / I've had enough
    of you / a swollen bag of useless opinions like all the old
    sods like you.

PEARL: Don't aggravate your father / his ulcer's killing him / go
    to bed / wash your face and go to bed / you don't look well,
    son.

MIKE: Ma / you've tied yourself to a lump of concrete / and it's
    sinking into the swamp.

PEARL: And who's complaining?

MIKE: I am!

PEARL: Don't worry about me / go to bed.

MIKE: OK.

    (MIKE *exits*.)

SID: Tell him in the morning to go / he's got to go / I for one
    can't take any more / so tell him / Pearl he's our son / but
    he's got to get out of this house / I can't take any more
    of it.

PEARL: I'll tell him.

SID: Make sure you do.

PEARL: I will / I said I will.

SID: He's got to go somewhere and do something / but I don't want him around any more / I'm sorry.

PEARL: In the morning I'll tell him to go.

SID: Don't soften up and change your mind.

PEARL: I'll tell him it's best for all of us if he went.

SID: You'll tell him that.

PEARL: Yeah.

SID: 'Cause this can't go on like this.

PEARL: I know that.

SID: Then we can have a bit of peace in our old age.

PEARL: Yeah.

SID: You know what I mean.

PEARL: Of course / I'll tell him in the morning / I'll tell him he must find somewhere else to live and not come back this time.

SID: I did my best.

PEARL: Yeah.

SID: Didn't I? . . . You sound as if I didn't well / didn't I or not / did I show him those ways?

PEARL: No, I did.

SID: What you talking about?

PEARL: From me he saw that not to fight was to give in / he saw that I never fought back / so he had to.

SID: You'll tell him in the morning to go!

Epilogue.

MIKE: I can't go on like this / look at me / my nose is out of joint / I can't see straight / I've got no job to speak of but I won / I won / I beat the beast / with my own two hands alone / I reached out and defeated what they feared / I conquered my own doubts when sick inside / that's great / so tell me where to go and what to do / and what's the trick that makes for happy days and nights / the fireside and mates around for Xmas / the wife cooking a bird / a baby

going gaga / the colour telly on / the Daimler shining round
the front / what did you do to get it / do you thieve / stay
on at school / or work your loaf / inherit some cosy chunk
of loot from papa / go on tell me the trick / what's the clue
I need to know some answers / or I'll make my own / you
who sit comfortably at home / who wake up with a grin and
toast and eggs / tell me what you do and how you do it /
never mind I'll find out / I'll get the wind on you / I'll
break out of this maze / and sniff around your pen / I'll be
the beast you fear / until I get an answer / straight up I
will / you had me do your dirt / and stood around to gape /
while I put down the fears that kept you sleepless in your
beds / there'll come another beast / for every one you kill /
there will grow another head.

Further epilogue.
PEARL *and* SID. GANG *as respectable people stand behind them.*
SID: Don't you worry / we did what we could / he's not so bad /
    a little wild / but soon he'll find his head / and if he don't /
    well then / others will help / there are the courts / police
    and magistrates to guide him on the way / prisons to help
    persuade / and keep society safe / so all in all he's no real
    threat to you and me / we keep our noses clean / pay the
    rent and rates / smile our social smile / and leave when they
    call time.
PEARL: But he's your son.
SID: No son of mine.

Blackout.
Faces of characters.

GREEK

AUTHOR'S NOTE

Greek came to me via Sophocles, trickling its way down the millenia until it reached the unimaginable wastelands of Tufnell Park – a land more fantasized than real, being an amalgam of the deadening war zones that some areas of London had become. Tufnell Park was just a word to play with – like our low comedians play with the sound of East Cheam for example – so no real offence to the inhabitants.

In my eyes, Britain seemed to have become a gradually decaying island, preyed upon by the wandering hordes who saw no future for themselves in a society which had few ideals or messages to offer them. The violence that streamed through the streets, like an all pervading effluence, the hideous Saturday night fever as the pubs belched out their dreary occupants, the killing and maiming at public sports, plus the casual slaughtering of political opponents in Northern Ireland, bespoke a society in which an emotional plague had taken root. It was a cold place in my recollection, lit up from time to time by the roar of the beast – the beast of frustration and anger, whose hunger is appeased by these revolting scraps, which momentarily dull its needs. We were the world's greatest video watchers, since we had lost the ability to speak to each other. We sat like zombies, strangled in our attempts to communicate, feeding off the flickering tubelike patients wired to support systems.

Oedipus found a city in the grip of a plague and sought to rid the city of its evil centre represented by the Sphinx. Eddy seeks to reaffirm his beliefs and inculcate a new order of things with his vision and life-affirming energy. His passion for life is inspired by the love he feels for his woman, and his detestation of the degrading environment he inherited. If Eddy is a warrior who holds up the smoking sword as he goes in, attacking all that he finds polluted, at the same time he is at heart an ordinary young man with whom many I know will find identification. The play is also a love story.

In writing my 'modern' *Oedipus* it wasn't too difficult to find contemporary parallels, but when I came to the 'blinding' I paused, since in my version it wouldn't have made sense, given Eddy's non-fatalistic disposition, to have him embark on such an act of self-hatred – unless I slavishly aped the original. One day a friend gave me a book to read which provided an illumination to my problem in an almost identical situation. The book is called *Seven Arrows* by Hyemeyohsts Storm. It contains a passage of such tenderness and simplicity that I was immediately given the key to my own ending:

'How is it, Hawk,' I asked him, 'that I should not make love to Sweet Water, my mother?'

'Do you love her?' he asked me.

I answered, 'Yes, more than anyone else . . . But . . . children of such a love are born wrong.'

'Have you ever seen one of these children?' asked Night Bear.

'No, I have not. And I have never known anyone who has.' . . .

'Then it is like everything else . . . It seems an easy thing to hear when a son kills someone, even his mother, but it is hard on people's ears when they hear of a son loving his mother.'

Greek was first performed at the Half Moon Theatre, London, on 11 February 1980. The cast was as follows:

EDDY and FORTUNE-TELLER	Barry Philips
DAD and MANAGER OF CAFE	Matthew Scurfield
WIFE, DOREEN, and WAITRESS 1	Linda Marlowe
MUM, SPHINX, and WAITRESS 2	Janet Amsden
Director	Steven Berkoff

Greek was transferred to the Arts Theatre Club, London, in September 1980. The cast was as follows:

EDDY and FORTUNE-TELLER	Barry Philips
DAD and MANAGER OF CAFE	Matthew Scurfield
WIFE, DOREEN, and WAITRESS 1	Linda Marlowe
MUM, SPHINX, and WAITRESS 2	Deirdre Morris
Director	Steven Berkoff

A new production of *Greek* was presented at Wyndham's Theatre, London, on 29 June 1988.

Place: England
Time: present
Stage setting: kitchen table and four simple chairs. These will
    function in a number of ways. They can be everything one
    wants them to be from the platform for the SPHINX to the
    café. They also function as the train; the environment
    which suggests EDDY's humble origins becoming his
    expensive and elaborate home in Act Two. The table and
    chairs merely define spaces and act as an anchor or base for
    the actors to spring from. All other artifacts are mimed or
    suggested. The walls are three square upright white panels,
    very clinical and at the same time indicating Greek
    classicism. The faces are painted white and are clearly
    defined. Movement should be sharp and dynamic,
    exaggerated and sometimes bearing the quality of seaside
    cartoons.

ACT ONE

SCENE I

EDDY: So I was spawned in Tufnell Park that's no more than a
stone's throw from the Angel / a monkey's fart from
Tottenham or a bolt of phlegm from Stamford Hill / it's a
cesspit, right . . . a scum-hole dense with the drabs who
prop up corner pubs, the kind of pub where ye old ass
holes assemble . . . the boring turds who save for Xmas
with clubs . . . my mum did that . . . save all year for her
slaggy Xmas party of boozy old relatives in Marks and
Sparks' cardigans who stand all year doing as little as they
can while they had one hand in the boss's till and the other
scratching their balls . . . they'd all come over and vomit
up Guinness and mum's unspeakable excuse for cuisine all
over the bathroom, adjust their dentures . . . rage against
the blacks, envying their cocks, loathe the yids envying
their gelt . . . hate everything that walks under thirty and
fall asleep in front of the telly . . . so they'd gather in the
pubs, usually a smelly corner pub run by a rancid thick as
pig shit paddy who sold nothing but booze and crisps in
various chemical flavours to their yokel patrons who played
incessant games of cruddy darts, drink yards of stale gnat's
piss beer and chatter like, 'see Arsenal last week . . . I
think England's team's all washed up . . . what abaht the
way he dribbled the . . . nah nah, he's lorst his bottle . . .
do leave orf . . .' the stink of the pub rises and the OAPs sit
in the corner staring out into the dreams they never had
with a drip of snot hanging off the ends of their noses and
try to make a pint last four hours . . . start crowding up
now and the paddy starts raving fucking time and pulling
the glass out of your hand while he's bursting your
eardrums screaming like a sergeant major his wife attempts
to shovel some paint on her evil hate-all face which looks as
if it's been applied by a drunken epileptic on a roller
coaster . . . ''allo luv', she foams . . . staring out of a

145

yellow face with little snot-brown eyes like two raisins in a plate of porridge. And if by chance you lean over the bar too far some bastard monster cunt Alsatian leaps at you, its dripping fangs simply dying to rip your fucking throat out . . . so I gave up going to the corner pub with its late night chorus of lurchy 'g'nights and see ya Tell' we got wine bars now, handsome.

That's much better – sit down, a half bottle of château or Bollinger, some pâté and salad by a chick who looks as if she's been fresh frozen . . . you take your favourite women there, my woman, very nice mate, looks like she's been just minted and sharp as new mown grass, knickers as white as Xmas, eyes like the bluest diamonds / a pair of fiery red rubies for lips, the light hits them and shatters your eyes, she smiles and your heart leaps into your throat and you carry a demon between your thighs and up to your chin / the whole time . . . I wear shades to protect myself against the brightness of her teeth . . . no tobacco stains on them boy . . . breath like an ocean breeze on Brighton Pier . . . now could you take her to that pub? Could you ever! Nah! It's really for the old fascists singing war songs on the pavement and 'Knees Up Mother Brown'. So I go to my wine bar with my bird who's carved out of onyx and marble and laced in the smells of the promise of sex the way you wouldn't believe . . . I swim in her like I was plunging into the Jordan for a baptism. So anyway one day my dad calls me in the kitchen. Come in son, he says, I wanna chat to ya, or we could go down the corner to the pub, I'll buy you a drink. No! not that pub I yelp in real and unfeigned terror. I'll throw some tea into a pot instead . . . mum's out . . . the Daily Mirror crossword half finished . . . well it is a bit grotty but homely in a sickly sort of way if you're not used to anything better it's not like the interior of a Zen temple but cosy. A few crumbs on the carpet, some evil photos of my sister on the mantelpiece and a picture of granny looking like Mussolini in drag

which they all looked like in those far off days of pre-history, the poodle's shit again behind the cocktail cabinet
. . . the old bacon rinds sit stinking in the pan and the room renches of lard. I made dad a cuppa. Mum's at bingo and sis is meditating in the bedroom on the squeezing out of some juicy blackheads . . . her old knickers lie sunny side up . . . she always left them on the floor for mum to scoop up while I wouldn't have touched them except with those pincers that pick up radium behind thick walls. So we sit down and he confesses this story to me . . . pulls out a fag and sits there with his flies half undone, and the ash of his fag ready to drop all over his shirt. I try not to look at him or his flies. I try to occupy my thoughts with my latest Stan Kenton. I look out of the window and see the grey clouds of Tottenham stray across the window pane
. . . a tiny sliver of sun is struggling to peep through sees what it has to shine on and thinks 'fuck it – is it worth it' and beats a retreat. So dad says, 'look here, son' I says 'yes, dad' clocking his work-raped face, his tasteless shit-heap Burton ready-made trousers and his deadly drip-dry shirt that acquires BO faster than shit attracts flies . . . I clock all this fusion of rubbish and say 'yes, dad? what do you want to chat abaht', never hearing much else out of his gob than 'send the darkies back to the jungle' and 'Hitler got the trains running on time' . . . you got a lot of Nazi lovers among the British down and out. Lazy bastards wondered why at the end of a life of skiving and strikes Moisha down the road copped a few bob or why the Cypriots had a big store full of goodies not that pathetic shit heap down our street that flogs only Mother's Pride mousetrap cheese a few miserable tins of pilchards and Heinz baked beans and a dreary cunt inside saying, 'no, we don't get no demand for that' when asked for something only slightly more exotic than Kelloggs. So dad did not come out with any of that fascist bullshit which relieved me since the Front were full of dads like this and that cunt in the grocery shop . . .
'yeah dad' I said 'what's on your bonce' . . . his face

squeezed up like it's hard to say, like those old ads for Idris
lemon squash showing a screwed-up lemon and comes out
with . . .

SCENE 2

DAD: When you were a nipper / we went to a gypsy, a fortune
teller / bit of a giggle / an Easter fair / don't laugh / a caper
what else / spent a tosheroon on a bit of a thrill don't talk
to me about thrills / so in we went / the gypsy asks 'have I
a son?' 'I have' I says, I mean who don't have a son? His
face meanwhile staring into the ball / his eyes all popping /
I'm not taking it for gen, straight up a lark / Easter and
all / I've got a lovely bunch and all that / his face gets all
contorted and twisted and he says / he sees a violent death
for this son's father / do what! but I'm his dad / come orf
it / don't get all dramatic / we get on like houses blazing /
and I see he says, something worse than death / and that's a
bunk-up with his mum / I'll give you a backhand I utter /
you're having me on / you been smoking them African
Woodbines / no he shrieks I see it, and what I see I see / so
don't pay me, just scarper / leave my tent / keep your gelt /
outside we ran, your mum was white as Persil / I as yellow
as a Chinaman with jaundice / course we took no notice /
forgot about it like, but not quite / waited till you got to be
a bloke and then one day I said Dinah / you remember that
darkie in the fair who came out with all that filth about
Eddy, one morning in bed just lying there, redigesting bits
of past and sucking still the flavour of some juicy memories
. . . 'not many' our Dinah slurps . . . 'not many, I nearly
dropped Doreen with whom I was six months pregnant
then / funny times' . . . well I say, that fair is back in
town, the same firm fifteen years later . . . let's bowl down
and see that geezer, tell that Hornsey gypsy what a lot of
old bollocks / how he upset my missus with his pack of
dirty lies / so off we went / doubted somehow that he'd

still be there, since he was pushing sixty then / you never
know, we waited our turn / it was the same name 'have
your future read / Fantoni's magic crystal gazer' . . . shall
we go in? . . .

MUM: . . . do you think we should? . . .

DAD: Why not, it's now or never / we went pale a bit but in we
marched / same old schmutter on the table, the beads we
walked through and the bit of old glass and no, it weren't
him, so I said where's the old geezer that we once saw
whose handle now you seem to have / 'my late old man' /
he said / 'five years ago he uttered his last / and fell off the
perch / but taught me the trade / imbued his vision in me /
I got his powers now / so don't you fret / if he did good by
you / donate a quid and I'll do my best' / . . . so Ed, your
mum and I sat down just like before / the years they shrank
away / just like a hole fell out the earth and time and space
had faded away / we seemed then to have hurtled back
those fifteen years / in that small tent / the music tinkling
through from the carousel outside and that funny smell /
the shouts growing faint just the whiff of stale grass under
our feet / and like the tent seemed small / like a trap and
suddenly hot and nothing outside just quiet but his face /
his face getting all twisted up just like his dad / his mouth
all white and tight like an earthquake was going on inside
his nut and his lips were straining against it coming out /
Dinah sussed but natch we waited / don't tell me I said you
see a son of mine / his eyes looked up affirmed / no word
just that look and his tight mouth / like holding back
something worse than vomit / 'and you see something
worse', I says, 'like a nasty accident perhaps' . . . He
nodded, parted his lips enough to mouth the word death
which he hadn't the guts to sound. He then stared hard at
Dinah / but we had enough and wanted not to hear the
other half but fled / I turned and snatched the quid back
from the table / don't know why / but like before when I
got my money back / it seemed to say by taking back the
gelt that it couldn't happen / his eyes looked like pity / like

those sweet pics you get in Woolie's of those kids with a
tear just ripe to drop / I know it's just a fun fair Ed / a
laugh, a bit of a giggle / I didn't blame the kid / what do
you make of it son / you don't fancy your old mum do you
son! You don't want to kill me do you boy.

DOREEN: Leave off you two.

EDDY: Doreen! His face hung there like a soggy worn out
testicle / mouth open and eyes like carrier bags / fancy my
mum! I could sooner go down on Hitler, than do anything
my old man so gravely feared / no dad / but all this aggro
and old wives' tale gone and put you in a tiz / I'll leave
home / split and scarper / the central line goes far these
days and that's to foreign climes / I'll piss off tomorrow / I
needed to escape this cruddy flat and this excuse seemed
good as any / tata ma and pa. They waved to me outside
the flats . . . my mum looked sad / her spotty apron
wrapped round her like the flag of womanhood / I never
saw her out of it / always standing in the kitchen like some
darkie slave behind dad and me and sis . . .

DAD: Bung us the toast.

EDDY: Where's the jam?

DOREEN: Pig!

MUM: More tea love?

DAD: Bung us the toast.

EDDY: Where's the jam?

DOREEN: Pig!

MUM: More 'taters love?

DOREEN: I'm on a diet.

MUM: More cake love?

EDDY: No mum I've had six slices already.

MUM: Go on have some more.

EDDY: I don't want no more you rancid old boot.

DAD: Hey!

EDDY: I'd spray affectionately.

MUM: Oh he don't like my cake.

EDDY: She'd simper . . . all right bung us another slice and I'll
wedge it down wiv a mug of tea to slop it up a bit and she

gazes at us with moist eyes on all of us slurping like fat pigs
in a trough / we'd leave a wreck-filled table, ma's washing
up, how well she knew that washtop / dad's picking out
losers in the worn out armchair – sis is fitting in her cap for
the night's activity cussing and swearing in the next room
as she struggles with it . . .

DOREEN: Fuck it!

EDDY: And mum sits in front of the box watching some dozy
cretin making cunts out of the cunts who go on to win a
few bob / mum's giggling in her glee / her legs like a
patchwork quilt from hogging the electric fire, while I was
in my little room plotting and dreaming of ruling the
world / take a Charles Atlas course / wondering if the
queen gets it often / or planning a dose of robbery wiv
violets or glorious bodily charm / so in my little room I
plotted smoked / played Stan Kenton and wanked wiv
mum's cooking oil. Now no more will I escape to my little
domain . . . hearing the sounds of hughy phlegm in the
next room through the snot-encrusted walls. So all in a
flash these thoughts slinked like maggots through my bonce
as I waved my goodbyes to the fast diminishing figures of
my mum and dad wed together in the distance like mould
on cheese . . . my dad was the mould / never mad about
him . . . as I reached the end of the road I could only see
the apron and lost the figure / the apron stayed in my mind
the longest. When my old lady went to the happy hunting
ground I would frame that apron.

MUM: Take good care of yourself.

DAD: Don't forget to write.

DOREEN: Got your photo.

MUM: Be a good boy.

DAD: Send us some money.

DOREEN: Miss yer.

MUM: Love yer Ed.

DAD: Take care on the roads.

DOREEN: Au revoir.

MUM: 'Bye, boy . . .

SCENE 3

DAD: The toast is burnt.

MUM: Saw Vi the other day.

DAD: Neighbours don't complain no more.

MUM: Matilda's had six kittens.

DAD: Where's my smokes?

MUM: 'Ere, 'ave you seen the cooking oil?

DAD: I miss our little Ed.

MUM: How will he fare strikes up and down the country.

DAD: The City sits in a heap of shit.

MUM: Of uncollected garbage everywhere.

DAD: The heat waves turn it all to slime and filthy germs hang
thickly in the air / the rats are on the march.

MUM: Transport sits idly at the docks where workers slink
around and for a hefty bribe may let you have your avocado
or Dutch cabbage . . . petrol's obsolete as thousands of
rusting cars lay swelling up our streets to vital services like
ambulances which take a month to get from place to place.

DAD: The country's in a state of plague / while parties of all
shades battle for power to sort the shit from the shinola /
the Marxists and the Workers' party call for violence to put
an end to violence and likewise the wankers suggest hard
solutions like thick chains and metal toecaps / Poisoned
darts half-inched from local taverns / anyone who wants to
kill maim and destroy / arson, murder and hack are being
recruited for the new revolutionary party / the fag libs are
holding violent demos to be able to give head in the public
park when the garbage strike is over and not to be
persecuted for screwing on the top deck of buses.

MUM: Forte's catering is resisting the staff's demand to be paid
wages and is recruiting workers from the jungles of South
America.

DAD: Yet also strongly resisting the need to clear out the rats for
which they are duly famous.

MUM: Most of the stores are closed but Fortnum's and Harrods

soldier on shrilly packed with screaming advocates of
limited nuclear drop on Hyde Park and so rid the country
they say of a twisted bunch of rancid and perverted filth.

DAD: The nights in Hyde Park are lit by fires and the sound of
tom toms from the Brixton black workers revolutionary gay
lib join forces with white is ugly forced abortion / wanking
is not a town in China but an alternative to the filthy men
female party group.

MUM: Meanwhile the rats head down Edgware Road up to
Oxford Street preparing to turn right into Bond Street / get
down Piccadilly and raid Fortnum's, pick up their mates at
Forte's and join forces to make all resistance impossible
seeing how all resistance is locked in internecine strife.

DAD: The rats march across Piccadilly avoiding Soho where the
food is dangerous even for rats, heading down to the
Strand / collect the Savoy contingent, overfat rats not sleek
for battle but just good germ carriers with rotten teeth head
across Waterloo Bridge and the National Theatre . . . try to
wake the theatre rats who have been long in coma from a
deadly attack of nightly brainwash.

MUM: Those that can be woken will begin the number two
division and streak up Drury Lane to Holborn and on to
King's Cross . . .

DAD: Avoiding the carcasses of rotting football Scots swollen
and putrefying on the streets / those who failed to make the
train and died while waiting for the next one / their flesh is
deadly / the rats come marching in.

MUM: Maggot is our only hope love.

DAD: If we only had more maggots to eat through the stinking
woodpile. But how is poor Ed going to manage in all
this? . . .

SCENE 4

EDDY: The shit has hit the fan as if from a great height / I
walked and walked / the sirens like wailing banshees from

black marias tear along the garbage-filled London streets,
chock full of close-shaved men in blue and clubs in black /
stacked full of teeth hate-clenched / wiv fists all hungry for
their daily exercise . . . the Scotties line the kerb face down
in vomit which swishes down the rat-infested gutters . . .
dumb jocks down for their dozy game of football / some
excuse to flee their fat and shit-heap Marys in the
tenements / they wear funny little hats with bobbles on and
rotten teeth, they belch into the carbon air their rotgut
fumes and sing a lurchy tune or two about owning some
pox-ridden scab-heap called Glasgow when they don't
own a pot to piss in. Then one blue-eyed bobby lays a
skull or five (well aimed, son) wide open. SMASH . . .
SPLATTER . . . CLOBBER . . . take that you tartan
git . . . CRASH . . . SHATTER . . . lovely . . . 'ere
you, wot the fuck you doin' . . . shut up . . .
KERACKKKK!!!!

family

The whores descend and drain their filthy wallets. With
their con of fuck and as the jock steps inside for fantasies of
London pussy. KERACK! a villain hard faced doth
distribute a bit of sense with bars of iron / so on they go,
the foul ignoble mob / they watch the match the wrong way
round so pissed as newts and then they stagger into Euston
station driven by a blind sense of instinct or smell to join
their fellow tartans on their journey back. 'Ay 'ad a loovely
taime.'

Meanwhile and spewing up the Mall down which I walked
to escape the deadly gas from ten-day haggis freshly heaved
upon our silver London streets. When what do I espy but
fuck and shit Macdougal and his paddies from Belfast and
raring to blow up anything that moves. Thick-eared with
hands like bunches of bananas / their voices from afar were
like a pack of baying hounds. They were an army dressed
in blue serge suits and without exception pale blue eyes and
liquid gelignite stuffed in their macs and little bombs in

* HATE HATE FROM THE BOMB
  x2

innocent sandwich bags . . . armpits concealing stinking
sweaty guns ready to blow some mother's son's head off
and spray the dusty Strand with thick rich ruby / knock off
some chick who God forbid could be some sweet of mine /
or take the legs off some poor cunt who happened to be
hanging about / and then they get all stinking in their pubs
and roar with leprechaunish glee . . . 'I've only got six
Guinnesses' . . . and fight to say who was the one to toss
the bomb . . . 'whose round is it now? How many tommies
did you spray apart? . . . my fucking husband's in the pub
again' . . . How many boys were drowning in their blood /
who that very night had kissed the loving girls
farewell . . . 'Jesus, Mary and Joseph' . . . How many
mothers' daughters copped a face of shrapnel / lost an
eye . . . 'Fuck my fucking husband, fuck it! . . .' How
many mothers douse the graves of kids of eighteen / wives
and widows chatting to a piece of earth while you, you
crock of gonorrhoea in serge wolf back another gallon, leer
home to your Bridget alone and waiting with six kids and
unwashed climb aboard dragging across her fleshy wastes
your skimpy shred of dirty prick / poke it about a bit and
come your drip of watery spunk ten seconds later / she's
lying there like a bloated cow / never known what coming
is / only read about those soft explosions in the groin /
heard rumours like / the only explosions paddy here can
make are ones that make you scream in fucking agony and
pain awash in blood not ecstasy and spunk. What a fucking
obscenity that is . . . FUCK FUCK FUCK AND SHIT /
MY FUCKING HUSBAND'S LYING ACROSS THE
ROAD / HIS LEGS ON ONE SIDE AND HIS TORSO
ON THE OTHER. OH GOD HELP ME. OH MAGGOT
SCRATCHER HANG THE CUNTS / HANG THEM
SLOW AND LET ME TAKE A SKEWER AND JAB
THEIR EYES OUT / LOVELY / GREEK STYLE /. . .

Hanging's no answer to the plague madam / you'd be
hanging every day / I'm human like us all / we're all the

same linked / if you kick one his scream will hit my ears
and hurt my mind to think of some poor cunt in shtuck /
the way a kitten crying in the night will make you crawl
out of your soft pit say what the fuck's up little moggie /
free Guinness that's the answer and sex instruction initiated
by luscious English birds well trained in fuck and suck
then instead of marching down the street with weapons of
war and little people on the side waving flags / they'll
march down with cocks at full alert and straining proud
and strong / and promptly get arrested. Still you can't help
it / you're drowned in aggro since a kid and dad has fed
between your flappy lugs not love but hate / has fed the
history of ye old past to give you causes / something to do
at night / has woven a tapestry of woe inflicted on him from
the distant foggy patch called past. So what else can you
do / your tired soggy brain awash with Guinness laced with
hate . . . I jumped into the bushes and watched the curly
mob in a storm of dust go past . . . the palace was on alert
. . . the sturdy chiselled chins fresh shaved of our fine and
brave John English ready to defend the queen and all her
minions who represent all that is fine in this drab of grey /
this septic isle . . . (*Chorus of 'Rule Britannia, Britannia
rules the waves . . .' etc . . .*) eventually got on a train /
found one whose carriage wasn't entirely smashed and
wrecked and rode in peace to London's airport skidrow
alone and reflective in my thoughts except for some Paki in
the carriage getting a right kicking for some no doubt vile
offence like inadvertently catching the eye of some right
gallant son of Tottenham, the kicking lent a rhythmic ritual
to my thoughts which were beginning to get formed to take
some mighty fine decisions that would shoot me on my
path to riches and success sweet smelling pussy and golden
arms and lashing tongues. I fell into a kind of reverie . . . I
fell asleep and dreamed . . . I saw a dozen pussies on a bed
nestled between some soft and squeezy thighs, like little
gentle kittens suckling on a mother's teat / their sweet and
ivory columns hanging loosely fell apart revealing flowers in

a garden that you water and like a randy bee I buzzed from
one to tother / their petals gently opened wide / sent forth
their perfumes in the air / and as I left they'd close again /
and then the next and each one subtly different / each like
precious luscious plants / each like a grasping toothless
mouth hungry like open beaks of little birds while I, like
mother, into their open throats would drop my worm
which hungrily and devouringly they'd grasp. Then I
awoke / and rudely saw the world just as it is and started
on my adventures thrust all young and sweet into the
seething heaving heap of world in which I was just a little
dot. (*Chorus of airport sounds and noises.*) All this confused
me / who needs to go / do I do you do he / I decided to stay
and see my own sweet land / amend the woes of my own
fair state / why split and scarper like ships leaving a sinking
rat / I saw myself as king of the western world / but since I
needed some refreshment for my trials ahead, I ventured
into this little café . . . everywhere I looked . . . I
witnessed this evidence . . . of the British plague.

SCENE 5

Café. Chorus of kitchen café menu sounds and phrases.

EDDY: One coffee please and croissant and butter.

WAITRESS: Right. Cream?

EDDY: Please. Where is the butter so I might spread it lavishly
and feel its oily smoothness cover the edges of the
croissant?

WAITRESS: Ain't got none. There's a plague on.

EDDY: Then why serve me the croissant knowing you had no
butter?

WAITRESS: I'll get you something else.

EDDY: I'll have a cheesecake, what's it like?

WAITRESS: Our cheesecakes are all made from the nectar of the
gods mixed with the dextrous fingers of a hundred virgins
who have been whipped with bull rushes grown by the

banks of the Ganges.

EDDY: OK. I'll have one.

(*She brings it*)

. . . I've finished the coffee now and won't have any liquid to wash the cake down with.

WAITRESS: Do you want another coffee?

EDDY: Not want but must not want but have to / you took so long to bring the cake that I finished the coffee so bring another . . .

WAITRESS: OK.

EDDY: But bring it before I finish the cheesecake or I'll have nothing to eat with my second cup which I only really want as a masher for the cheesecake.

WAITRESS: OK. (*To another waitress*) . . . so he came all over your dress . . .

WAITRESS 2: Yeah.

WAITRESS: Dirty bastard.

WAITRESS 2: It was all thick and stringy it took ages to get off / he was sucking me like a madman when my mum walked in.

WAITRESS: No! What did she say?

WAITRESS 2: Don't forget to do behind her ears / she always forgets that.

WAITRESS: I wish my mum was understanding like that / I haven't sucked a juicy cock for ages, have you?

WAITRESS 2: No, not really, not a big horny stiff thick hot pink one.

WAITRESS: What's the biggest you've ever had?

WAITRESS 2: Ten inches.

WAITRESS: No!

WAITRESS 2: Yeah, it was all gnarled like an oak with a great big knob on the end.

WAITRESS: Yeah?

WAITRESS 2: And when it came, it shot out so much I could have wallpapered the dining room.

EDDY: Where's my fucking coffee? I've nearly finished the cheesecake and then my whole purpose in life at this particular moment in time will be lost / I'll be drinking hot coffee with nothing to wash it down with.

WAITRESS: Here you are, sorry I forgot you!

EDDY: About fucking time!

WAITRESS: Oh shut your mouth, you complaining heap of rat's shit.

EDDY: I'll come in your eyeballs you putrefying place of army gang bang.

WAITRESS: You couldn't raise a gallop if I plastered my pussy all over your face, you impotent pooftah bum boy and turd bandit.

MANAGER: (*Her husband*) What's the matter, that you raise your voice you punk and scum / fuck off!

EDDY: No one talks to me like that.

MANAGER: I just did.

EDDY: I'll erase you from the face of the earth.

MANAGER: I'll cook you in a pie and serve you up for dessert.

EDDY: I'll tear you all to pieces, rip out your arms and legs and feed them to the pigs.

MANAGER: I'll kick you to death and trample all over you / stab you with carving knives and skin you alive.
(*They mime fight.*)

EDDY: Hit hurt crunch pain stab jab

MANAGER: Smash hate rip tear asunder render

EDDY: Numb jagged glass gouge out

MANAGER: Chair breakhead split fist splatter splosh crash

EDDY: Explode scream fury strength overpower overcome

MANAGER: Cunt shit filth remorse weakling blood soaked

EDDY: Haemorrhage, rupture and swell. Split and cracklock jawsprung and neck break

MANAGER: Cave-in rib splinter oh the agony the shrewd icepick

EDDY: Testicles torn out eyes gouged and pulled strings snapped socket nail scrapped

MANAGER: Bite swallow suck pull

EDDY: More smash and more power
MANAGER: Weaker and weaker
EDDY: Stronger and stronger
MANAGER: Weak
EDDY: Power
MANGER: Dying
EDDY: Victor
MANGER: That's it
EDDY: Tada.
WAITRESS: You killed him / I never realized words can kill.
EDDY: So can looks.
WAITRESS: You killed him / he was my husband.
EDDY: I didn't intend to I swear I didn't / he died of shock.
WAITRESS: He was a good man, solid except in his cock but he
was good to me, and now I am alone / who will I have to
care for now. Who to wait for at night while he cleans up
our café or while he's at the sauna getting relief / who to
cook for or brush the dandruff from his coat and the grease
from his hat or the tramlines from his knickers / who to
comfort in the long nights / as he worries about me / who
will put the kids to bed with a gentle cuff as he frolics after
coming home all pissed from the pub and smashes me
jokingly on the mouth / whose vomit will I clean up from
the pillow as he heaves up all over my face on Friday nights
after his binge. Whose black uniform will I press in
readiness for his marches down Brixton with the other so
noble men of England / whose photos will I dust in the
living room of his heroes, Hitler, Goebbels, Enoch, Paisley
and Maggot not forgetting our dear royals. Is it worth it
any more? / I married a good Englishman / where will I
find another like that? See what you did / and all over a
stupid cheesecake.
EDDY: Wars, my dear, have been fought over less than that.
WAITRESS: I'll never find another like him.
EDDY: Yes you will.
WAITRESS: Where?
EDDY: Look no further mam than this / your spirits won me /

cast thy gaze to me / my face / and let thine eyes crawl
slowly down / that's not a kosher salami I'm carrying / I'm
just pleased to see you / sure I can do like him / polish my
knuckleduster / clean **my** pants / I'll give you a kicking
with the best if that's what you really want / you'll have my
set of proud photos to dust / I'd rather treat you fair and
square and touch your hair at night and kiss your sleeping
nose / I'll not defile your pillow, but spread violets beneath
your feet / I'll squeeze your toes at night if they grow cold
and when we through rose gardens walk I'll blow the
aphids from your hair / I'll come straight home from work
at night not idle for a pint and all my spunk I'll keep for
thee to lash you with at night as soft and warm as summer
showers / I'll leak no precious drop in the Camden sauna
for a fiver ('don't be long dear, others waiting') but strew
the silver load in thee to dart up precious streams / I'll
heave my sceptre into thee / your thighs I'll prise apart and
sink like hot stone into butter / into an ocean of ecstasy for
that's what you are to me / an ecstasy of flesh and blood
and fluted pathways softest oils and smells never before
uncapped / I'll turn you upside down and inside out / I'll
strip you bare and crawl under your skin / I'm mad for
you / you luscious brat and madam, girl and woman turned
into one / I'll kiss your bum hole like it was the lips of
cherubs / I'll take you love for what you are!

WAITRESS: You've eased my pain you sweet and lovely boy / I
thought I'd miss him desperately but now I can when
looking at you hardly remember what he looks like. You
look so familiar to me though we have never met / so
strange perhaps the true feeling love brings to your heart.
The familiar twang.

EDDY: I feel the same for you.

WAITRESS: You remind me of someone or something.

EDDY: What, ducky?

WAITRESS: Oh, nothing.

EDDY: Confess my dear the quandary that doth crease your
brow and makes the nagging thought stay in your head, the

way an Irish fart hangs in the air long after its creator
wends his weary way to Kilburn High Street.

WAITRESS: 'Tis nothing sweet but this / I had a kid, just two he
were, sweet and blue-eyed just like you / a darling, then
one day disaster struck / and don't it just / an August trip
to Southend for the day / all hot and sticky with floss and
smiling teeth / hankies and braces / start off at Tower Pier
excitement, sandwiches and loads of fizzy Tizer.

EDDY: (*Aside*) Strange, I love Tizer.

WAITRESS: Then two or three miles out we hit a mine that
slunk so steadily up the Thames, like some almighty turd
that won't go down no matter how often you flush the
chain, so this had stayed afloat, it showed its scarred and
raddled cheek from its long buffets round the choppy seas
and just by luck as if the fates had ordained us to meet it
blew us at the moon / at least it made a hole so large that
suddenly the Thames resembled Brighton on a broiling day
with heads a-bobbing everywhere, my Frank swam back
and I clung to a bit of raft but little Tony, for that was his
fair name, ne'er did surface up . . . I hope his end was
quick.

EDDY: No chance that some local fisherman may have snatched
him from the boiling seethe.

WAITRESS: No word, no sign, not even his little corpse did
show / I stuck around all night, then as the dawn arose I
saw his little oil-soaked teddy bear, as if heaved up from
deep inside the river's guts. It lay amidst the condoms on
the junk-filled strand. I took it home and washed it.

EDDY: That's a sad tale / and I feel grieved for you my dear that
woe should strike at one who was so young and fair / and
let the others more deserving of fate's lash to get away with
murder.

WAITRESS: Fate never seems to give out where it's meant but
seems to pick you out as from a hat / like bingo and if your
number's on it boy you've had it.

EDDY: That little bear you mentioned, sweet . . . may I see the
precious relic.

WAITRESS: You really want to?

EDDY: Yeah, let's have a butcher's.

(*She goes and brings the bear in.*)

'Tis strange but often times I dreamed of such a thing a
little Rufus just like this / I never had one, yet seemed to
miss the little furry cuddly thing as if my body knew the
feel whereas my mind could not / since then I've always
liked small furry things. Come, love, you've had your share
of woe and so have I and if fate heaps the shit it also heaps
the gold and finding you is like a vein I never dreamed of,
so fate's been kind this time / I think we're fated, love
don't you?

WAITRESS: I do, my precious, for once I bless the stars that this
time made me such a man / you've got the same eyes as my
Tony – green and jadey like the sea.

EDDY: Your eyes are like the sunlight in the sea that speckles on
the rocks so deep below / all blue and gold.

WAITRESS: Your face is like all Greek / and carved from ancient
marble.

EDDY: Your body feels all soft like puppies, strong as panthers.

WAITRESS: Let's go to bed my sweet.

EDDY: OK.

DAD: Do you think that it could happen
that the curse could come about
that Ed could kill his own dad,
pop into his mother's pants, I had to kick him out.

MUM: That's something we will never know dear
until the day, when suddenly you'll
see quite a different Ed than the one that's known to me.

DAD: You're right, dead right . . . oh Dinah
what did we do that such a curse
should be blasted on the heads of me and you.

MUM: Who knows my dear what evil lies in store
that we are unaware of, did we cause some
grief somewhere, inflict some unhealed sore.

DAD: I've done nothing all my life
I've been an honest Joe

163

shit on that fortune teller
and his vile and evil joke.

MUM: It's funny that twice we heard it Ted
it's funny that a second time
another face years later should
sound the same old horrid warning line.

DAD: Perhaps we should have told him Dinah
perhaps we ought to tell
our son should know the secret
or we may end up in . . .

MUM: Hell you mean, you make me laugh
it's over now, it's past,
it can't be now undone with words
fate makes us play the roles we're cast.

ACT TWO

SCENE I

EDDY: Ten years have come and gone, scattered their leaves on
us / drenched us in blazing sun and rain / toughened my
sinews to combat the world. I improved the lot of our fair
café by my intense efforts, aided of course by my sweet
mate / got rid of sloth and stale achievement / which once
was thought as normal / I made the city golden era time /
the dopes just died away when faced with real octane high-
power juice / the con men that have tricked you all the
while with substitute and fishy watery soup / went out of
business and people starved for nourishment brain food and
guts just flocked to us / the fat-faced bastards you saw
sitting on expense accounts and piles / too long defied the
needs of our gnawing biting hunger / real food and drink /
real substance for the soul / not those decayed and spineless
wonders who filled the land / strutting and farting pithy
anecdotes at boring dinner parties on profits made by con
and cheap / they thought they were the cream and not the
sour yuk they really were / we showed them the way / they
died in trying to keep up with us / they faded in a heap.

WIFE: Ten years have flown away as Apollo's Chariot hath with
fiery stride lit up our summers, thawed our frosts and
kissed our cheeks / ten winters hath the hoary bearded god
of ice encased our earth in pinch hard grip of chill / to be
kicked out in turn by spring's swift feet of Ceres, Pluto,
Dionysus / and April brooks do glisten giggling over rocks
and reeds so pleased to be set free / ten years this splendid
symphony of life hath played its varied song / hath
saddened and elated / hath drawn the sap of life into the
fiery poppy and frangipani and gripped them in its autumn
sleep again / whilst we my man that is and me, for three
thousand three hundred and sixty-five times did celebrate
our own ritual in nights of swooning.

EDDY: While I each day and year have scored another niche into

this world of ours / have moved about and jostled / cut a
throat or two metaphoric of course and shown how what
this world doth crave is power, class and form with a dab
of genius now and then. We cured the plague by giving
inspiration to our plates / came rich by giving more and
taking less / the old-style portion control practised by fat
thieves went out with us / we put the meat back into the
sausage mate / now once more the world will taste good /
no more the sawdust and preservative colouring and cat
shit that you could better use to fill your walls than line
your stomachs / so foul that nations overseas would ban
them from their fair stalls and shops lest their strong youth
should fall into the listless British trance so often seen in
Oxford Street or on the Piccadilly line at 8 a.m. / a nation
half asleep and drugged with foul and bestial things poured
out of packets / massed up by operators who conspired
with commies thick in plot to weaken our defences / feed
the nation shit and mother's crud and watch them crumble
down in heaps upon the pavement / then the cunning reds
just blow them over skittle-like / but now in our great chain
we energize the people, give soul food and blistering blast
of protein smack / sandwiches the size of fists chock full of
juicy smile-filled chunks / the nation blinks and staggers
back to work on this / not fast / it takes a while to use those
muscles starved so long / limp with only holding *Daily
Mirror* race results / and eyes so dim from weekly charting
of the pools / we'll get them back to work, no fear though
they may die of shock upon the way / we'll drag them out
of pubs, their fingers still gripping on the bar they know so
well, like babies reluctant to part with mother's tit / it's us
that has to do it / rid the world of half-assed bastards
clinging to their dark domain and keeping talent out by
filling the entrances with their swollen carcasses and
sagging mediocrity / let's blow them all sky high, or let us
see them simply waste away as the millions come to us.
(*Chorus sing 'Jerusalem'.*)

The SPHINX.

WIFE: The plague is not quite over yet. There's still a plague
around this city darling that will not go away, caused by
some say some evil deed that has not purged itself, but
continues to rot away inside the wholesome body of our
state / people are dropping like flies / armed killers snipe
from the shattered eyes of buildings and death stalks in the
foul and pestilent breath of friends whose eyes are drunk
with envy and greed at your success / people shake your
hand with limp grips as if afraid to catch it. The illness of
inertia, and should I shan't I, the country's awash in
chemicals that soup the brain to dullness to dull the
dullness of grinding hips long bored with ancient habit and
lovers are afraid to stroke each other's groins lest new laws
against the spreading the plague outlaw them.
Masturbating shops line every High Street and the
pneumatic drill of strong right wrists ensures a girl a fat
living, the country's awash in spunk not threshing and
sweetening the wombs of lovers but crushed in Kleenex
and dead in cubicles with red lights. Meanwhile men in
white masks are penetrating the holy crucible where life
may have slipped in, and armed with scapels and suction
pumps tear out the living fruit and sluice it down the river
of sewage, the future Einsteins, Michelangelos and future
Eddys. The blood and plasma of creation is swept and
flushed away with gasps of 'don't' inside the tender
packages not yet fulfilled.
EDDY: That's the plague at work all right, there's something
rotten in the city that will not die / a sphinx I read stands
outside the city walls tormenting all that pass they say and
killing those who cannot answer her strange riddle / no
doubt she helps to spread the canker and the rot and yet no
one can destroy her.
WIFE: I heard that too, and yet she can at will dissolve herself to
air.
EDDY: I'll go and sort her out.
WIFE: Be careful darling / you are all I have.

EDDY: Don't fret, if I've come this far, survived the worst that
fate can throw I'll come through this as well don't wait up I
may be late but if I'm not back by dawn, I'll meet you in
heaven, if not we'll meet in hell!

SCENE 2

SPHINX *outside the walls*.

SPHINX: Who are you, little man / pip squeak scum / drip off
the prick / mistake in the middle of the night / you've come
to answer my riddle / the riddle of the sphinx / fuck off you
maggot before I tear your head off / rip your eyes out of
your head and roast your tongue / you nothing, you man /
you insult of nature go now before I lose my cool.

EDDY: I'm not afraid of you . . . you old slag / you don't scare
Eddy 'cause Eddy don't scare easy / I've beaten better than
you in Singapore brothels / you can only frighten weak men
not me / why do you exist to kill men you heap of filth /
you detestable disease / because you can't love / loveless
you can only terrify man no one could love you / who could
even kiss that mouth of yours when your very breath stinks
like a Hong Kong whorehouse when the fleet's in.

SPHINX: You make me laugh you fool man / you should know
about brothels, they exist for you to prop up your last
fading shreds / men need killing off before they kill off the
world / louse, you pollute the earth / every footstep you
take rots what's underneath / you turn the seas to dead
lakes and the crops are dying from the plague that is man /
you are the plague / where are you looking when you
should be looking at the ghastly vision in the mirror / the
plague is inside you. You make your weapons to give you
the strength that you lack / you enslave whip beat and
oppress use your guns, chains, bombs, jets, napalm, you
are so alone and pathetic, love from you means
enslavement, giving means taking, love is fucking, helping

is exploiting, you need your mothers you mother fucker, to
love is to enslave a woman to turn her into a bearing cow to
produce cannon fodder to go on killing / can you ever stop
your plague / you're pathetic, unfinished, not like me,
never like us, a woman, a sphinx. Women are all sphinx. I
have taken the power for all, I am the power / I could eat
you alive and blow you out in bubbles / I devour stuff like
you . . . oh send me strong men you scrawny nothing /
look what they send me / mock up heroes / plastic movie
watchers / idolizer of a thousand westerns / punk hero /
flaccid man / macho pig / rapist filth and shit / oh nature's
mistake in the ghastly dawn of time / when women were
women, androgynous and whole and could reproduce
themselves but somewhere and some time a reptile left our
bodies, it crawled away and became man, but it stole our
little bag of seed and ever since the little reptile has been
trying to crawl back, but we don't want it anymore, all we
need is your foul little seed, you gnat . . . something that
takes you thirty seconds of your life and us nine months we
create build nourish care for, grow bigger and fat and after
we suckle and provide. While you dig in the earth for
treasure, play your stupid male games / go you biped of
dirt / just a prick followed by a heap of filth, I feel sorry for
you / I really feel for you / I've eaten enough men this
week / so go / fuck off / stink scum dirt shit / go, before I
tear you to pieces / go and plot and scheme, hurt, exploit
and rape, oppress and wound, make a few more evil laws
you shrivel of flesh, you poor unreliable penis. You have
not even our capacity for passion . . . I could come ten
times to your one / wanna try big boy? You are from my
rib mister / me from you? what a joke / woman was Adam /
she was the earth, woman is the tide / woman is in the
movement of the universe / our bodies obey the phases of
the moon . . . our breasts swell and heave and our rich
blood surges forth to tell us we are part of the movement of
nature / what signs do you have? / How do you know that
you are even alive? / Do you bleed / do you feel the kicking

in your womb / does a mouth draw milk from your soft breast / can you tell the future / can you do anything? What signs do you have / a date with death / the hour you must attack / unable to create you must destroy / I am the earth / I am the movement of the universe / I am liquid, fire and all elements / my voice rises octaves high and communicates with the spirits of the dead / my skin is soft and velvet and desirable to those with rough faces and bodies hard and muscled to labour, to toil across the face of the earth for us / the goodness of life / woman / we / sex / sphinx, the grand and majestic cunt, the great mouth of life / the dream of men in their aching lonely nights / the eternal joy that men die for and envy and emulate / what they sicken for and crave for and go insane for / so go, you are small, insignificant, piss off you worm or I'll break your teeth and pull out your fingers / go fuck yourself or stick a bomb up your fucking asshole you heap of murdering bastard shit filth . . . go, you make me vomit.

EDDY: Without me you are nothing / without me you wouldn't exist without me you are an empty screaming hole.

SPHINX: You what! You think I need you. I need milk but do I go to bed with a cow. I'll farm and fertilize you and keep you in pens where you will do no harm / now go boy, I am getting aroused, be grateful that for some reason I feel for your pathetic attempts at heroism.

EDDY: I want to answer your riddle.

SPHINX: Then you must know that those that can't answer it die, and then if you can't I will kill you, I will tear your cock off with my teeth before I eat you up.

EDDY: With pleasure / if I answer it / what do I gain.

SPHINX: You can kill me.

EDDY: Then I will cut off your head for women talk too much.

SPHINX: I agree. You're a brave little fart. So here goes: what walks on four legs in the morning, two legs in the afternoon and three legs in the evening?

EDDY: Man! In the morning of his life he is on all fours, in the afternoon when he is young he is on two legs and in the

evenings when he is erect for his women he sprouts the
third leg.

SPHINX: You bastard, you've used trickery to find out the
riddle.

EDDY: No, just reason. All right, sorry to have to do this, I was
growing quite fond of you.

SPHINX: I don't care any more / to tell the truth I was getting
bored with scaring everyone to death and being a sphinx /
OK cut it off and get it over with.
(*He cuts off her head.*)

SCENE 3

EDDY: She would put you off women for life / but not me / I
love a woman / I love her / I just love and love and love
her / and even that one / I could have loved her / I love
everything that they possess / I love all their parts / I love
every part that moves / I love their hair and their neck / I
love the way they walk across the kitchen to put the kettle
on / in that lazy familiar way / I love them when they open
their eyes in the morning / I love their baby-soft skin / I
love their voices / I love their smaller hands than mine / I
love lying on them and them on me / I love their soft
breasts / I love their eyelashes and their noses / their teeth
and their shoulders / and their giggles / and their desperate
passions and their liquids and their breath against yours in
the night / and their snores / and their legs across yours and
their feet in the morning and I love their bellies and thighs
and the way each part fits into mine / and love the way my
part fits into them / and love her sockets and joints and ball
bearings / and love her hip bone and her love-soaked parts
that want me / I love her seasons and love her sleeping and
love her walking and speaking and whispering and loving
and singing and love her back and her bum nestled into
you and you become an armchair / and love her for taking
me in / and giving me a home for my searing agonies / my

lusts / my love / my dreams / my sweetness / my honey /
my peace of mind / and love pouring all my love into her
with open eyes and love our fatigue and love her knees and
shoulder blades and pimples and love her waiting for me
and love her soothing me as I tell her about my day's
battles in the world – and love and love and love her and
her and!

(WIFE *enters*.)

WIFE: Well done my sweet, now all will be well / my hero . . .
yes you are / my brave and shining knight / my lion, yes!
And I'm your mate / my brave and gentle lion / and now to
celebrate let's have your dear old pa and ma to dine and
reconcile the fairy tales and woes of past and be all gooey
nice together in family bliss.

EDDY: I have to laugh when I think of my soppy mum and
dad / locked up in council bliss / and £40 a week driving a
38 from Putney down to Waltham Cross and getting
clobbered each Saturday night.

WIFE: Invite them over Ed, to share just once our colour TV,
hi-fi, home movies showing us in fair Ibiza and Thebes, of
you diving in the bright blue cobalt sea, your smiling new-
capped teeth all sparkling in the brilliant sun, invite them
to partake of our deep leather sofas / succulent wines /
show our video that records those programmes that you
wish to view when after working late at night in selfless
graft you sit with dog and slipper by your feet . . . let them
enjoy the comfort of central-heated bathroom . . . no more
the cold ass on a plastic seat but wool-covered and pipes all
steaming hot, of stairs thick-gloved in pile so soft that each
tread is like a luscious meadow. Would they not like a
Slumberdown or even our soft waterbed which thrusts our
pelvises so sweetly swished together, needlepoint shower
show your mum the joys of kitchen instant disposal waste,
no washing up, just time to enjoy our super apple pie.

EDDY: I'll send the chauffeur down to pick them up / that's if
my dad has rid himself of that old hoary myth that like a
louse ate inside his nut, to tell him of patricide and horrid

incest / or subtitled could be called the story of a mother
fucker / a tale of kiddiwinks to send them mad to bed and
cringe at shadows in the night, and in their later years to
bung good gelt to shrinks in Harley Street.

WIFE: When you told me that story Ed / I could not believe that
grown ups still could set such store by greasy gypsies in a
booth / and to kick you out all young and pink into the
seething world while you were wet behind the lugs / maybe
'twas a ruse to get you out the nest.

EDDY: Who knows my dear the wily minds of cruddy mums
and dads whose heads chock full of TV swill, the pools and
read your own horoscope / who believe in anything they
read that comes so fluent forth from out the gushy asses of
the turds in Fleeting Street / so what, it put me on the
springboard young and lively and I learned how to jack
knife into the surging tide with all the best.

WIFE: You're tuf that's what my love / you're a survivor in the
swilling mass of teeth and knives and desperate eyes all
anxious to carve out their pound of flesh / you did it and
you're still a beaut / still lovely brown and svelte / success
has not paunched you or stuck a fast ass on your hips or
burnt an ulcer in your gut / or made your mouth a stinking
ashtray where fat cigars hang like a turd that cannot be
expelled / but hangs on till the end / your sweet and honey
breath / your tongue's not coated with the slime of ten-
course meals taken with other con artists who flash their
gaudy rings and thick as pig shit wives who sit at home and
wank or play some bridge with other dozy bags whose only
exercise is stretching out an arm to screech out 'taxi'
outside Harrods / you're sweet and your body's like a river,
flowing, flowing, flowing into me / it moves like a flowing
river . . . your streaming muscles carry me along your
river, along your soft and hard and flowing river / when
I'm in your arms I'm carried along this endless stream and
then I reach the sea, I'm swept up by your sea, I'm carried
by a wave, I'm threshed up in your wave and then set
down again only to be re-gathered up as your volcanic wave

GREEK

gathers me as a piece of ocean, as your sweet lustful pangs
gather up its morsel I'm swept up, I'm gathered up, I'm
sucked up and spun along a raging storming river . . . I
love your body, I love your fingers and round and round
and tearing and gripping and finding and searching and
twisting and gathering me for your sweet lustful pangs . . .
and then and then and then . . . your body is like a tree
. . . like branches twisting and breaking . . . like a wave
like a wind, like an animal like a lion . . . ferocious and
sweet lustful pangs grow bigger darling . . . as they grow
bigger to make your sweet spunk flow . . . they grow
bigger and the lion's breath is hot and the grip on me is
growing tight and more ferocious and then and then I know
. . . that you tremble, you shake, you quiver, you thrash
. . . oh the river flows, oh . . . it flows, oh it floods through
me . . . as you tremble your quiver is shot into me . . . oh
I am flowing with the river in the wet and warm and
succulent flow . . . you turn me into a flow and flood me
. . . and the shivering and the quivering and the shaking
and the trembling, softly softly . . . softly goes as the storm
passes slowly . . . goes . . . slowly . . . rumbling into the
distance . . . slowly goes the breath less hot, but soft and
silky and sweat on your back and silky on your thighs and
warm between our thighs . . . oh / life my love / oh love
my precious / oh sweet my honey / oh heaven my angel / oh
darling my husband.

EDDY: But soft my darling wife / what noise is that / it must be
my cruddy mum and dad / who interrupt your lovely flow
of gob rich thick and pearly verbs that send my blood a-
racing to my groin so I might manufacture love-wet tides.

SCENE 4

MUM *and* DAD *enter*.
DAD: Look how he's got on / you really got on well son / I'm
proud of ya. He's got class and qualities drawn from me.

174

MUM: From me more, his mum whom he did love not this wet
fart that calls himself his dad.

DAD: Don't talk like that in front of Eddy's wife you sloppy
titted, slack-assed lump, you raving scrawny dried-up
witch.

MUM: Don't talk to me about my body / age has withered my
soft beauty but you will need cremating since your
poisoned flesh would cause pollution in the earth and make
widespread crop failures / you're death on two varicosed
legs and a hernia belt.

DAD: I've got no words for you Dot . . . since you were gang-
banged by that bunch of drunken darkies . . . a dozen it
were, if I counted right, whose swollen truncheons flashed
their golden sprints of foam into the sulphurous and heavy
night, since that bad time you've not been right in ye old
bonce . . . I know that night was dark for you in double
horror and I fear that it may be the cause of your unseemly
evil tongue that like a poisoned snake doth linger under
filthy damp and rotting stone.

EDDY: Hallo dad, hallo mum – good to see ya again . . .

MUM: Oh Ed, it looks really lovely, and this is your lovely wife /
oh! how lovely, oh, she's nice.

WIFE: Why thank you, I think you're very charming yourself.

MUM: Oh thank you. You are nice, have a nice day, you're
welcome.

WIFE: Please feel free, make yourself at home, how very nice to
meet you. Have you had a good journey? How is everyone
at home? Isn't the weather cold now. It will soon be winter.
You're looking so young. You really look well. You've lost
weight. Are you going away this summer? Do you use
Fablon in your kitchen?

MUM: You've a lovely home, it's really lovely, just lovely. Some
people are lucky, some people have all the fun. Some
mothers do have 'em. Mind you, I mean, it goes to show,
well it does. Idle hands make wicked thoughts. He's all
right, really, underneath . . . when you get to know him,

he's lovely, have you been away this year? Water off a
duck's back, dear.

EDDY: So what's the news my folks / my flesh and blood / chip
off the old / apple of your / say what goes on in my old
neighbourhood / where once rank violence stalked the dirty
streets and filthy yobbos hung round the corners of old
pubs like flies on dead carrion / say can you still walk down
the streets at night? Or do you macaroni in your pants at
every shadow that stalks out lest it be some Macdougal out
to line his coat with other's hard-earned gelt . . . around
this manor there's peace my folks. Move out that council
flat where urchins' piss does spray the lift which takes you
to your eyrie on the twenty-fifth floor and move in with us,
or do you still fear that old curse / that bunch of gypsy
bollocks, that you so avidly did gulp / though secretly me
thinks you used that as a ruse, to clear me out the womb
and save yourself some L.s.d. / you always said I'd eat you
out of house and home / round here only the poodles drop
their well-turned turds in little piles so neat. And au pair
girls go pushing little Jeremys into the green and flowery
parks / no ice-cream vans come screaming round this
manor / all's quiet / just the swish on the emerald lawns
close cropped like the shaven heads of astronauts / and in
the quiet of the evening silly chit chat from the strangled
vocal cords of well-heeled neighbours rises from the
gardens as they wolf down in the summer nights a half a
dozen gin and tonics. Nicely tired from a hard day's graft
of thieving in the city. So come and stay. You're welcome
and bring the cat as well, we've always got room for
moggie.

DAD: Nah son but thanks and double ta. You're very kind to us
. . . how thoughtful / bless you, you're welcome, have a
nice day, but we're used to wot we got, can you teach an
old dog new tricks, a bit long in the tooth you're as old as
you feel, and I feel like a worn out old fart . . . we know
the familiar faces / our rotten neighbours / the geezer who
collects the payments on the fridge and on the telly every

week / meals on wheels that daily calls now that we're
getting older, all familiar trappings that have trapped us /
now that our useful working life has been sucked dry by
the state we get a little pension and some security for which
I sign / now that my boss god bless him sits back fat and
greasy / not that I mind, he got it by hard graft and
cunning / good luck to him / he gave me fifty quid when I
retired, handsome and a watch with fifteen jewels / right
proud I was / so what I got asbestos in my lung / so what I
got coal dust in my blood / so what I got lead poisoning in
my brain / so what I got shot nerves from the machines / so
what I lost two fingers in the press / so what I'm going deaf
from the steel mills / so what I lost a lung for our old king
in Dunkirk / I'd do it again / yes I would I tell ya / so what
I got fuck all for it from our fair state / so what they're
gliding past in their Rolls-Royces / and their fat little kids
come tumbling out on piggy little legs / so what they thieve
and murder and get away with it / so what our lovely royals
pay no tax / they're figureheads mate / so what I starve
waiting for your cheque which sometimes you forget to
send if you are busy entertaining, when you forget your old
ma and pa . . . son!

MUM: Don't listen Ed, he's gone a bit in the nut since they
retired him / all he does is grouse and quail. When you
complain remember others worse off than you / I think of
mothers whose sweet fruit of their most holy wombs / those
warm and precious sacks of giggling joy, who have been
snatched by sex-mad fiends. They stalk around the town
. . . . there are so many around / you cannot pick up the
daily snot-picker these days without seeing between the tits
and race results the photos of the burns and scalds and
broken limbs . . . the staring eyes of kids / how one is
burnt by fag ends / others punched black and blue /
screams in the night / neighbours too scared or fastened to
Hawaii Five-O to receive the bloated cries that stab
through the walls like an open hand saying help me /
others, babies with broken lips, their little ribs all smashed

by dads who have caught the British plague that cements
their heads and puts vitriol inside their hearts / some kids
chained to their beds for hours at a time and others
crawling in shit and piss . . . and whack and zunk goes
mum and splatter back hand crack goes dad . . . one kid's
nipples almost burnt off . . . what about the dad who
picked up his small innocent and smashed his head against
the wall, until his brains seeped out . . . what dreams did
that kid have as his grey thoughts ran down the wallpaper
. . . and then the judge says . . . 'off you go, you are
basically a good character' . . . and then he's off to
celebrate in the nasty pub with his old lady . . . and up and
down the length and breadth the straps are out and babies,
bairns and kids are straightened out, lashed out, whipped
and made to obey, the nation's full of perverts if you ask
me / the plague still flourishes mate.

EDDY: The plague mum / the plague is still about? You never
did nuffin like that to me / you only gave me muffins and
jam / swaddles of lovey love and spoiling and playing and
story-telling. And swishing my pillow and a ride on dad's
back and chase around the garden, and a three-wheel bike.
You only gave me ten slices of toast every morning and
Marmite after school . . . I looked all Bisto like, and like
those kids whose shoes have a long way to go I was put on
a path called bliss with jammy mouth and sticky doughnut
fingers / a dad who put me on the crossbar of his bike and
never once introduced the back of his hand to my bonce
not once opened his eyes wide and hate-filled and sought to
venge some filthy taste for colouring my flesh in Chartreuse
green or bruisy blue. No! We'd race across the municipal
lido. How long can you stay under. *Dandy* and the *Beano*
each week and even the *Film Fun* as well.

DAD: You were loved son / we wanted to give you love / we
luved ya kid. You know . . . like open hands gripping your
shoulders and a squeeze at the end . . . palm on your head
and ruffling your hair, a clenched fist and a slow tap on the
chin . . . like chin-up when you didn't pass your eleven-

plus 'cause you were a dummy . . . I didn't want you to
hate us.

EDDY: Hate? I never used that word my folks, only pocket
money each week five bob and Sat morn flicks. Do you
mean to say you loved me because you were afraid I'd hate
you. 'Cause the gypsy's curse rang in your ears. Let's
smother him with spoiling and cuddling so he won't want
to hurt his old dad, you make me laugh . . . you would
have loved me the same without the rotten curse / I'm your
flesh and blood, it's natural.

DAD *and* MUM: But you're not our son, son.

EDDY: SHIT GIVE UP THE GEN / SPILL YOUR GUTS /
OPEN YOUR NORTH AND SOUTH AND LET ROLL
THE TURDS BEFORE I PONEY MY Y-FRONTS. IN
OTHER VERBS OPEN YOUR CAKE-HOLE AND
UTTER. LET ME EARWIG YOUR HOBSONS. NOT
YOUR SON. OH BOLLOCKS AND CRACKLOCK.

WIFE: Don't say that he ain't your real produce of your blood-
swept thighs, not shoved out of your guts in warm sticky
afterbirth, not the sparkle in his dad's eye in the glinting
night when his pa heaved apart his woman's limbs and
unloaded a binful of hot spunk, not eyed her like a
lodestone or a star, or a jewel in the corner of his eye not
breathed hard or pulse raced to produce this lovely hunk of
super delicious wondrous beefy darling spunky guy / not
seen you walking from behind and wanted to grasp your
arse and deliver the mail up your wet and wondrous
letterbox?

MUM: Nah! 'Fraid not!

WIFE: Oh fuck.

EDDY: So what if I'm adopted / who gives a monkey's tit.

DAD: Like this it was. Cries and groans, shouts and shrieks. I
was fishing by Wapping, just down from the *Prospect of
Whitby* . . . a peaceful Sunday (you were fished out, what a
find, what I prayed for, a son) threw my line, the big
steamers going out to Southend. The old Tower Bridge
opening up to allow the steamers' funnels through like

some big lazy East End tart from Cable Street opening her
thighs . . . on the deck in the sun the people of Bow,
Whitechapel and Islington in their cheese-cutters and
chokers, all doing a bit of a dance on the deck, the
streamers flickering, the Guinness pouring . . . us waving
from the shore as the old steamer cuts through the scummy
old Thames and sends the swell over to us and makes our
little boats kneel and bob as she passes by. When all of a
sudden boy / the sun's up high, Hitler's just topped hisself.
It's hot. Churchill's in command, there's peace at last.
Twenty million dead / including my two boys, the radio
plays we'll meet again and mares eat oats and does eat oats
and little lambs eat ivy, remember. Well all of a sudden in
that hot August afternoon no bananas in the shops and
coupons for four ounces of sweets each week, pictures of
Auschwitz just come out / thousands of bodies like
spaghetti all entwined / all done in the name of Adolf / all
of a sudden in the hot blue day . . . they're all swimming
look at them, look at all that blood and oil, bad mix, the
sky turned black. What a terrific hell of a bang, and soot is
dropping all over us plus bits of people, all the fish dropped
dead, from shock, hey let's shalp them out. Look let's get
some help, they're all in the water. Some jerry ball of hate
stacked full of painful promise and carrying the names of
the future dead blew the Southend tripper to the moon and
down they fell in a deadly mash of Guinness and Gold
Flake . . . come on mate . . . 'I'll give you a hand'. We
pulled them in all night, the others just bloated up like fun-
fair freaks. Come on mum, don't fret, 'ere have a cuppa,
where's your little Johnnie? . . . now, now he'll be all
right, can he swim? No . . . oh. We'll find him . . . won't
we lads . . . we'll find the little bleeder . . . shine your
torch over here Bert, yeah, there's an old lady, give us your
hand love, I'll pull you in . . . oh no, just a stump, she left
it in the water . . . what bastard could do this . . . more
blankets . . . bring more tea . . . there's just not enough of
us . . . there's not enough people to help, who does this to

people! What sick perverted bastard started all this shit
. . . if he was in front of me, I would take a butcher's
fucking knife and carve him slowly bit by fucking dirty
piece and feed it to the river rats and any cunt that
supports him, I'd fucking throw them in acid baths . . .
when all had gone and the dawn arose we saw what seemed
a little doll clinging to a piece of wood but on closer
butchering revealed a little bugger of about two he were,
struggling like the fuck and gripping in his paw a greasy
old big bear, which no doubt helped to keep him up. We
threw the bear back in the slick, and lifted the toddler out
all dripping wet and covered in oil looking like a darkie so,
no one about we took him home and washed him / he was a
beaut / and mum was double chuffed to see a little round
soft ball of warm goo goo / 'don't want to give him up'
quoth Dinah, 'must we' she said. 'Nah', I said 'his mum
will think he's dead anyway' / so let her go on thinking it /
but think our Dinah rightly slurps of how its real mum will
fret and pine and waste away and mourn for her sweet
lovely soft flesh of her own / 'all right' I says 'we'll keep
him for one day only and then give him back.' A day
turned into two / then after a week we thought the shock
now would be too great and that the true mum would be
adjusted to her sad loss.

WIFE: Oh shit and piss and fuck. I just pissed in my pants.
(*She faints.*)

EDDY: My dearest wife and now my mum, it seems, this lady
was the very one whose baby you snatched / she told me
the selfsame and bitter tale of how she lost her Tony and if
you found him then I am he, he whom you found that
belonged to her was me. The he you stole and gave to her
did once belong to she . . . nice to see ya, have a nice day,
so I am the squelchy mass of flesh that issued from out the
loins of my dear wife / oh rats of shit / you opened a right
box there didn't you, you picked up a stone that was best
left with all those runny black and horrid things intact and
not nibbling in my brain. So the man I verballed to death

was my real pop / the man to whom my words like hard-edged shrapnel razed his brain / was the source of me, oh stink / warlock and eyes break shatter, cracker and splatter . . . ! / Who laughs? Me who wants to clean up the city / stop the plague destroy the sphinx / me was the source of all the stink / the man of principle is a mother fucker / oh no more will I taste the sweetness of my dear wife's pillow . . . no more . . . no more . . . so I left my cosy and love-filled niche now so full of horror / foul incest and babies on the way which if they come will no doubt turn into six-fingered horrors with two heads / poor Eddy. Oh this madness twisting my brain / I walked through the plague rot streets and witnessed the old and the broken / the funny faces staring out of the dead vinyl flats / the flickering shadows of the TV tube / I sat in cafés and thought of my desirable lovely succulent and honey-filled wife and as I sat and stared at the rheumy faces and the dead souls with their real wives who were plastered forever in casts of drab compromise, my own wife seemed like a princess / I fastened her face on the horizon like the rising moon and stared forever into space / and when the café closed I sat and stared forever and forever, ran through in my mind every combination of her face and smile and eyes and twists and curves of her lips, I sat and projected her picture on the moon and pored through every page of our life together like a great holy bible of magic events I examined every feature of her landscape and ate up every part of her and loved every part whose sum total made up this creature, my wife. And then the moon turned as red as blood / the clouds raced across her face and became her hair and then her eyes and the wind pulled her hair over her face / like it did when we walked together through the fields and the forests, when the trees shivered and the sun kissed us and the universe wrapped us round in a cloak of stars and rain and crushed grass and ice-creams and teas and clenched fingers / hold on to me / hold on to me and I will hold on to you and I'll never let you go, hold on to me, does it matter

that you are my mother, I'll love you even if I am your
son / do we cause each other pain, do we kill each other, do
we maim and kill, do we inflict vicious wounds on each
other. We only love so it doesn't matter mother, mother it
doesn't matter. Why should I tear my eyes out Greek style,
why should you hang yourself / have you seen a child from
a mother and son / no. Have I? No. Then how do we know
that it's bad / should I be so mortified? Who me. With my
nails and fingers plunge in and scoop out those warm and
tender balls of jelly quivering dipped in blood. Oedipus
how could you have done it, never to see your wife's golden
face again, never again to cast your eyes on her and hers on
your eyes. What a foul thing I have done, I am the rotten
plague, tear them out Eddy, rip them out, scoop them out
like ice-cream, just push the thumb behind the orb and
push, pull them out and stretch them to the end of the
strings and then snap! Darkness falls. Bollocks to all that.
I'd rather run all the way back and pull back the sheets,
witness my golden-bodied wife and climb into her
sanctuary, climb all the way in right up to my head and
hide away there and be safe and comforted. Yeh I wanna
climb back inside my mum. What's wrong with that. It's
better than shoving a stick of dynamite up someone's ass
and getting a medal for it. So I run back. I run and run and
pulse hard and feet pound, it's love I feel it's love, what
matter what form it takes, it's love I feel for your breast,
for your nipple twice sucked / for your belly twice known /
for your hands twice caressed / for your breath twice smelt,
for your thighs, for your cunt twice known, once head first
once cock first, loving cunt holy mother wife / loving
source of your being / exit from paradise / entrance to
heaven.

12 Wensday cuffer